BORN TO DIE

BORN TO DIE

Cover

- *Old Wooden Cross* image by Cindy Micka Wright
  (www.glory4him.weebly.com)
- *Trusting Baby* image by Chuck Bagby
  (Corbin Bagby – Grandson of Chuck Bagby)

Available at
www.BurningHeartBibleStudies.com
(and most booksellers)

BORN TO DIE

The Jesus Story:
What I Wish I Had Known
(Book 1)

Chuck Bagby, PhD

BURNING HEART BIBLE STUDIES™

San Antonio, Texas, USA

Available at
www.BurningHeartBibleStudies.com
(and most booksellers)

© 2014 Charles E. Bagby, Jr.

First Edition

- First Printing March 16, 2014
- Second Printing June 1, 2014
- Third Printing September 1, 2014
- Fourth Printing February 16, 2015
- Fifth Printing May 1, 2015
- Sixth Printing October 1, 2015
- Seventh Printing June 1, 2016
- Eighth Printing December 6, 2017

Published in San Antonio, Texas by Burning Heart Bible Studies (www.BurningHeartBibleStudies.com). Burning Heart Bible Studies, the Burning Heart Bible Studies logo, Bagby Translation, and BT are trademarks of Burning Heart Bible Studies, Inc.

BT (Bagby Translation) designates a passage of Scripture translated by Dr. Chuck Bagby.

Scripture quotations marked NASU (New American Standard Bible Update) cite the New American Standard Bible® 1995 updated translation, New American Standard Bible® Copyright© 1960, 1962, 1963, 1968, 1971, 1972, 1973, 1975, 1977, 1995 by The Lockman Foundation (www.Lockman.org). Used by permission.

Photographs courtesy of the Library of Congress, Prints and Photographs Division, 101 Independence Ave. SE, Washington, DC 20540, USA, unless otherwise noted.

ISBN (International Standard Book Number) 978-0-9911520-0-1

LCCN (Library of Congress Control Number) 2013920119

To the grandchildren of Chuck and Robin Bagby,

May you forever use your talents to further Jesus' kingdom.

Kayley

Charlie

Demos

Zachary

Layla

Aravis

C.J.

Hana

Corbin

Samantha

Owen

Acknowledgements

Four years of weekly constructive critique from members of the Christian Writers Group of Greater San Antonio led to the transformation of *Born to Die* from rough draft to polished literature. I thank Brenda Blanchard, Richard Barnett, John Lovitt, Brian Veneklase, Mint Newman, Phillip Williams, Kelly McCoy, and Lill Kohler for helping me learn to write effectively.

I extend further gratitude to Dr. Paul McQuien and Al Brander. While Paul lent his linguistic expertise to ensure readers would not trip over grammatical obstacles, Al provided keen proofreading eyes to sweep the book clean.

Without the enduring patience and devoted support of my wife, I would have found it impossible to complete this first book of *The Jesus Story: What I Wish I Had Known* series. Robin, I love and appreciate you dearly.

Any glory drawn by this work I direct toward God, who by His grace prepared me to undertake the task at hand.

Contents

Preface

The road to wisdom? – Well, it's plain
and simple to express:
Err
and err
and err again
but less
and less
and less.[1]

I have daydreamed of going back in time while retaining what I now know about Jesus. Given that head start, I could have erred less, attained a more steadfast faith, and increased my productivity as His servant. Since I cannot return to the past to begin my journey anew, I will share what I wish I had known and optimistically spur your faith forward.

Matthew, one of Jesus' biographers, provides the story line as we explore the first 30 years of Jesus' life on Earth. When citing Matthew's

---

[1] "The Road to Wisdom," *Grooks*, by Piet Hein (20th- century Danish poet): The M.I.T. Press, Cambridge, MA 02142, U.S.A. (1967, p. 34)

book, *Born to Die* utilizes the *Bagby Translation* (BT),[2] a precise and reader-friendly rendering of Matthew's Greek[3] text. In addition, Mark, Luke, and John supplement the story with episodes from their biographies of Jesus.

Born to Die speaks clearly enough for a novice to understand, yet digs deeply enough to cultivate a believer's faith. You will discover little-known facts, as well as details hinted at by Jesus' original biographers, but never addressed by later writers. Sifting out unverifiable legend and myth, drawing solely on the Scriptures and other ancient historical sources, *The Jesus Story: What I Wish I Had Known* series will set you free to explore the authentic history of Jesus' life and teachings.

Enjoy the story and make up your *own* mind about Jesus. As His apostle[4] Paul urged the Christians in Rome,

The faith which you have,
have as your own conviction before God.[5]

---

[2] For more information about the Bagby Translation, see "Appendix 2: The Bagby Translation."

[3] The authors of the New Testament books and correspondence wrote their works in Greek, which served as an international language during the first century A.D. due to the enduring Hellenistic (Greek) influence of Alexander the Great's vast conquests three centuries earlier as he expanded his Macedonian Empire. By writing in Greek, New Testament authors effectually communicated within the Roman-Empire, as well as non-Roman Mediterranean cultures.

[4] Apostle – *transliteration* of the Greek word *apóstolos* (ă-pŏ-stŏ-lŏs), ἀπόστολος, a common Greek word describing any delegate. However, within the Scriptures it typically refers to the 12 followers chosen by Jesus to represent Him. See Luke 6:12-16 for a list of the twelve. When *transliterating*, a translator spells out an approximation of the original language's pronunciation of a word using the alphabet of the second language.

[5] Romans 14:22 NASU (New American Standard Bible Update, 1995 revision). For more information about the NASU, see the copyright page, which follows the title page.

CHAPTER 1

....

Jesus: God's Solution to Our Dilemma

Before humans – before Earth, before the moon, before the cosmos – only the spiritual realm existed. The Father, the Holy Spirit, and the Word (Jesus)[6] reigned as one God over the Kingdom of Heaven.[7]

God created a physical world to coexist with the spiritual realm.[8] In that new world, He placed the first man and woman in a garden paradise called Eden.[9] Adam and his wife Eve lacked nothing as they cared for the garden.[10]

In Eden stood the tree of life, which bore fruit that preserved human bodies from death.[11] The tree of knowledge of good and evil also grew among the vegetation, in the middle of the garden.[12] God warned Adam and Eve never to eat from that tree or they would lose their lives.[13]

---

[6] Revelation 19:13
[7] John 1:1-3; Colossians 1:13-17
[8] Genesis 1:1
[9] Genesis 2:7-8
[10] Genesis 2:15-16
[11] Genesis 2:9; Genesis 3:22-24; Moses wrote the text of Genesis 3:22 in the grammatical imperfect aspect of the Hebrew language, which indicates Adam and Eve ate fruit from the tree of life continually over time until God exiled them from Eden.
[12] Genesis 2:9; Genesis 3:3
[13] Genesis 2:16-17; Genesis 3:3

As Adam and Eve passed near the forbidden tree one day, its beauty drew Eve's attention.[14] Desiring the knowledge it offered, she picked its fruit and took a bite. She then handed the fruit to Adam who also ate it.[15]

They immediately understood the implications of their misbehavior and tried to hide from God among the trees.[16] True to His word, God drove the man and woman out of Eden, separating them from Him and the tree of life. He posted cherubs[17] to guard the way to the tree of life, ensuring neither Adam nor Eve could return to eat its fruit and enable their bodies to live forever.[18]

In addition to their eventual physical death,[19] Adam and Eve suffered a spiritual death the day God removed them from His presence. Likewise, God spiritually separated each of us from Himself the day we first rebelled against Him.[20] Nonetheless, aware of our tendency to do carelessly whatever we please, our loving Creator designed a selfless plan to deliver us from the dreadful consequence of our defiance.[21]

He would forgive us – conditionally. Only the compelling blood of an innocent man's voluntary self-sacrifice could bridge the chasm separating us from God's favor.[22] Hence, our dilemma – none of us could make amends for our own misconduct, much less for the wrongdoings of all humanity, because we all have disobeyed God.[23]

---

[14] Adam approached the forbidden tree "with her" (Genesis 3:6 NASU).

[15] Genesis 3:6

[16] Genesis 3:8

[17] Cherubs exist among the other spiritual-realm beings created by God. Instead of using the word cherubs, some translators have chosen to utilize *cherubim*, a transliteration of the Hebrew plural word of cherub. When transliterating, a translator spells out an approximation of the original language's pronunciation of a word using the alphabet of the second language.

[18] Genesis 3:22-24

[19] Genesis 5:5

[20] Isaiah 59:2; Ezekiel 28:15; Romans 5:12; Romans 6:16,23; Ephesians 2:1-2,11-16 (Note verses 1 & 12.); Colossians 2:13-14; 2 Thessalonians 1:5-10 (Note verse 9.)

[21] Matthew 10:28; Matthew 13:49-50; Matthew 25:41-43,46 (Note verse 46.); Romans 2:5-11; Romans 6:23; 2 Thessalonians 1:6-10 (Note verse 9.); 2 Peter 2:4-11 (Note verse 9.); Jude 4-14 (Note verses 6-7.)

[22] Hebrews 9:22; Leviticus 17:11

[23] Romans 5:12

To our rescue came Jesus, the Word of God.[24] While maintaining His godhood, the Word emptied Himself of the power and privileges of God to appear as a common human infant when born on Earth.[25] Born to die,[26] He made our reconciliation with God possible by offering *His* blameless blood as an acceptable sacrifice on our behalf.[27]

John, a beloved friend of Jesus, spoke on behalf of all the prophets who walked on Earth with Jesus when he wrote,

> *What was from the beginning, what we have heard, what we have seen with our eyes, what we have looked at and touched with our hands, concerning the Word of Life ... we proclaim to you also, so that you too may have fellowship with us; and indeed our fellowship is with the Father, and with His Son Jesus Christ.*[28]

Open your mind and open your heart as you consider in the following chapters – what I wish I had known about the Jesus story.

---

[24] Revelation 19:13

[25] Philippians 2:5-7; John 1:14

[26] Matthew 20:28; Mark 10:45; John 10:17-18

[27] 1 Corinthians 15:3; Hebrews 9:26-28; Hebrews 10:12; Isaiah 53:10; 1 Peter 2:24; 1 John 1:7

[28] 1 John 1:1-3 NASU

CHAPTER 2

....

Kings & Scoundrels: Jesus' Ancestors

Do you know your ancestry? Do black sheep pop up their heads in your lineage? Do you descend from anyone of fame?

The ancestors of the working-class family into which the newborn Jesus arrived consisted of kings and scoundrels. Matthew highlighted Abraham and David, both honorable men of Hebrew nobility, when he listed Jesus' forebearers. Yet, he also mentioned a few scandalous characters along the way such as Judah, Rehoboam, Abijah, Joram, and Uzziah.

God's Old Testament prophets foretold that the Deliverer (Jesus) would descend through Abraham,[29] as well as David.[30] With that in mind, Matthew launched his story by listing Jesus' genealogy to assure readers that His family line fulfilled prophetic expectation.

---

[29] Galatians 3:6-16 (Take special note of verse 16.); Genesis 22:15-18 (Take special note of verse 18.); Genesis 12:1-3

[30] Psalm 89:3-4; Psalm 132:10-11; Micah 5:2; Acts 2:29-30

Matthew's Text[31] (Matthew 1:1-17)[32]

1 A book about the life of Jesus Christ, a son of David, a son of Abraham.

2 **Abraham** *fathered Isaac,*

Isaac *fathered Jacob,*

Jacob *fathered Judah and his brothers,*

3 **Judah** *fathered Perez and Zerah through* **Tamar,**

Perez *fathered Hezron,*

Hezron *fathered Aram,* [33]

4 **Aram** *fathered Aminadab,*

Aminadab *fathered Nahshon,*

Nahshon *fathered Salmon,*

5 **Salmon** *fathered Boaz through* **Rahab,**

Boaz *fathered Obed through* **Ruth,**

Obed *fathered Jesse,*

6 **Jesse** *fathered David the king.*

David *fathered Solomon through* **Uriah's wife,**[34]

7 **Solomon** *fathered Rehoboam,*

Rehoboam *fathered Abijah,*

Abijah *fathered Asaph,* [35]

8 **Asaph** *fathered Jehoshaphat,*

Jehoshaphat *fathered Joram,* [36]

Joram *fathered Uzziah,*

9 **Uzziah** *fathered Joatham,*[37]

Joatham *fathered Ahaz,*

Ahaz *fathered Hezekiah,*

---

[31] The text quoted from Matthew's book comes from the Bagby Translation (BT). For a discussion of the BT, see "Appendix 2: The Bagby Translation."

[32] Luke 3:23-38 parallels Matthew 1:1-17. Neither Mark nor John contains a parallel passage.

[33] Some translators refer to Aram as "Ram."

[34] Uriah's wife – Bathsheba

[35] Some translators refer to Asaph as "Asa."

[36] Some translators refer to Joram as "Jehoram."

[37] Some translators refer to Joatham as "Jotham."

_10_ **Hezekiah** *fathered Manasseh,*
Manasseh *fathered Amos,*[38]
Amos *fathered Josiah,*
_11_ **Josiah** *fathered Jechoniah and his brothers during the Babylonian deportation.*
    _12_ *After the Babylonian deportation,*
Jechoniah *fathered Salathiel,*
Salathiel *fathered Zerubbabel,*
_13_ **Zerubbabel** *fathered Abiud,*
Abiud *fathered Eliakim,*
Eliakim *fathered Azor,*
_14_ **Azor** *fathered Sadok,*[39]
Sadok *fathered Achim,*
Achim *fathered Eliud,*
_15_ **Eliud** *fathered Eleazar,*
Eleazar *fathered Matthan,*
Matthan *fathered Jacob,*
_16_ **Jacob** *fathered Joseph,* **Mary***'s husband, through whom was born* **Jesus***, the One called Christ.*
_17_ *Altogether there were fourteen generations from Abraham to David, and from David to the Babylonian deportation were fourteen generations, and from the Babylonian deportation to the Christ were fourteen generations.* (BT)[40]

---

[38] Some translators refer to Amos as "Amon."

[39] Some translators refer to Sadok as "Zadok."

[40] BT (Bagby Translation) designates a passage of Scripture translated by Dr. Chuck Bagby. For more information concerning the Bagby Translation, see "Appendix 2: The Bagby Translation."

The One Called Christ (Matthew 1:1,16-17)

"A book about the life of Jesus Christ,"[41] Matthew boldly declared in his first sentence. *Christós* (khrĭs-tŏs),[42] the Greek word in the New Testament Scriptures[43] translated "Christ," means "Anointed One." *Mashíyach* (mâ-shí-yäkh),[44] the Hebrew word in the Old Testament Scriptures translated "Messiah,"[45] also means "Anointed One." Hence, Christ and Messiah serve as synonyms.[46]

What did Matthew intend his readers to understand when he referred to Jesus as the Anointed One?[47] What responsibilities did Jesus assume as "the One called Christ?" Watch for answers to those questions as you investigate the Jesus story.

Abraham (Matthew 1:1-2,17)

Son of Abraham

God's prophets of old indicated the Messiah's birth would occur through the bloodline of Abraham,[48] the ancestral patriarch of the Hebrew race. When calling Jesus "a son of Abraham,"[49] Matthew did not imply Abraham fathered Jesus directly, but that Jesus *descended* from Abraham, His ancestor.

---

[41] Matthew 1:1 BT

[42] *Christós* (khrĭs-tŏs), Χριστός; See "Appendix 4: Pronunciation Symbols."

[43] The prophets who composed New Testament literature wrote their books and correspondence in Greek. Prophets who penned the Old Testament books did so primarily in Hebrew, although they employed Aramaic in a few sections, specifically Jeremiah 10:11, Daniel 2:4 - 7:28; Ezra 4:8 - 6:18; Ezra 7:12-26.

[44] *Mashíyach* (mâ-shí-yäkh), משיח

[45] Daniel 9:25-26 provides two examples of translators rendering the Hebrew word *Mashíyach* as "Messiah."

[46] Synonymous words have the same meaning or nearly the same meaning.

[47] For a discussion regarding the anointing of Jesus by the Father, see "Chapter 10 – Jesus Fulfills All Righteousness," heading "Spirit of God Descending (Matthew 3:16)."

[48] Galatians 3:6-16 (Take special note of verse 16.); Genesis 22:15-18 (Take special note of verse 18.); Genesis 12:1-3

[49] Matthew 1:1 BT

History of Abraham

Abraham[50] grew up in Ur,[51] a coastal city in the land of Chaldea.[52] The discovery of certain cuneiform[53] inscriptions in the 1850s A.D. enabled archaeologists to identify the remains of Ur at Tel Muqayyar,[54] in southeastern Mesopotamia. A harbor city, Ur lay on the northern coast of the Persian Gulf during Abraham's era. Over the ages, the coastline withdrew southeastward, placing the ruins of Ur about 150 miles[55] northwest of the Persian Gulf and six miles[56] south of the Euphrates River.

Map: Ur

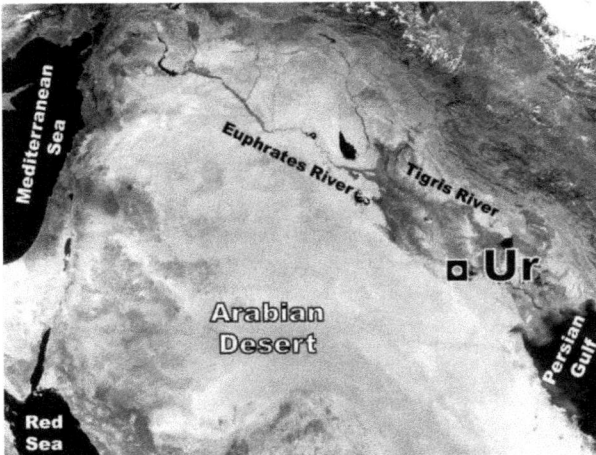

Figure 2 - 1

---

[50] Originally called Abram, God later changed Abram's name to Abraham (Genesis 17:5).

[51] Genesis 11:27-29

[52] Genesis 11:28,31; Nehemiah 9:7

[53] Cuneiform, a system of writing developed by the ancient Sumerian culture of southern Mesopotamia, emerged about 3100 B.C. For more information concerning cuneiform, see "Appendix 3: Glossary."

[54] A *tel*, an artificial hill created by the accumulated ruins of an ancient civilization, would grow increasingly larger over the centuries as successive generations built new structures on top of the mound.

[55] 240 kilometers

[56] 10 kilometers

Ziggurat of Ur (Temple of the Moon Goddess Nanna, 1932 A.D.)

Figure 2 - 2

Ruins of Ur (Looking from Top of Ziggurat, 1932 A.D.)

Figure 2 - 3

Ruins of Ur (1932 A.D.)

Figure 2 - 4

Ruins of Ur (Courtyard and Houses, 1932 A.D.)

Figure 2 - 5

Terah, Abraham's father, led a few members of his family away from Ur, intending to migrate to the land of Canaan.[57] A message God delivered to Abraham motivated Terah's decision to leave Ur, "Leave your country and your relatives, and come into the land that I will show you."[58] Abraham would have departed Ur prior to 2003 B.C., the year the Elamites conquered and destroyed the city.

Canaan lay several hundred miles of Ur, near the Mediterranean Sea. Traveling straight west to Canaan would have required crossing the Arabian Desert, not an enticing prospect. Instead, Terah chose to go around the Arabian Desert, leading his caravan to the northwest, along the Euphrates River.

He paused about 900 miles[59] into the journey, three-fourths of the way through the route. For an unexplained reason, Terah settled in the city of Haran, near the northernmost point of his proposed trek to Canaan.[60] Haran lay along the bank of the Balih River, a tributary of the Euphrates River. Although the Scriptures do not reveal how long Terah's family lived in Haran, he eventually died there.

Terah's Route from Ur to Haran

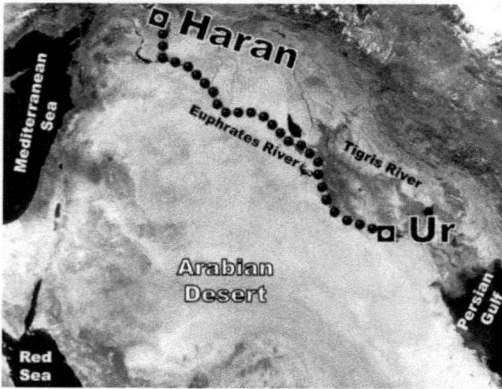

Figure 2 - 6

---

[57] Genesis 11:31
[58] Acts 7:2-4 BT
[59] 1,450 kilometers
[60] Genesis 11:31

During Abraham's stay in Haran, God again instructed him to relocate to "the land which I will show you."[61] With Sarah (his wife), and Lot (his nephew, whose father had died in Ur),[62] Abraham "went out, not knowing where he was going,"[63] taking along "all their possessions which they had accumulated and the persons which they had acquired in Haran."[64] God then led them to Canaan.[65]

Abraham's Route from Haran to Canaan

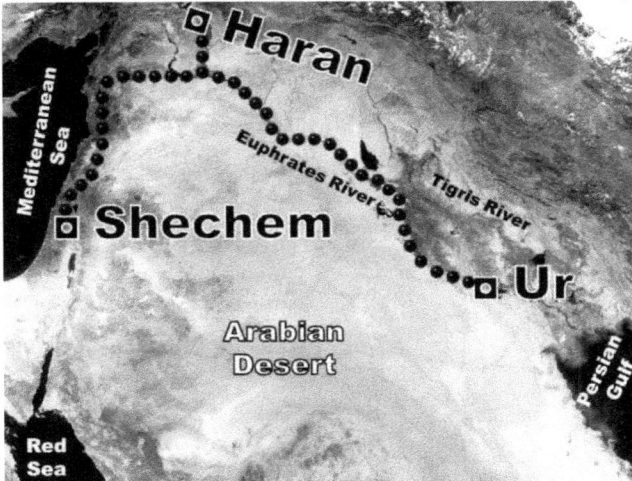

Figure 2 - 7

Following Abraham's arrival in Canaan, God tested his obedience, instructing him to sacrifice his son, Isaac.[66] Raising a knife over the altar to slay Isaac, Abraham's hands would have trembled as tears drained off his beard. Even so, Abraham maintained confidence in God's promise to build his descendants into a "great nation."[67] He trusted God to bring Isaac back

---

[61] Genesis 12:1 NASU
[62] Genesis 11:31
[63] Hebrews 11:8 NASU
[64] Genesis 12:5 NASU
[65] Genesis 12:5
[66] Genesis 22:1-18
[67] Genesis 12:2 NASU

to life in order to fulfill His word.[68] Before the knife slit Isaac's throat, God sent an angel to stop Abraham from completing the sacrifice.[69]

Due to Abraham's trusting works of faith, God declared him righteous,[70] and "he was called the friend of God."[71] Fulfilling His promise to make Abraham "a great nation,"[72] God ensured that Isaac's descendants flourished. The offspring of Isaac's son, Jacob, developed into the nation of Israel.[73] David, one of Jacob's descendants, became king of Israel.

---

[68] Hebrews 11:17-19

[69] Genesis 22:10-12

[70] James 2:21-24; Other Scriptures that discuss Abraham's faith include Genesis 11:26-12:6, Genesis 22:1-18, Acts 7:2-4, and Hebrews 11:17-19.

[71] James 2:23 NASU

[72] Genesis 12:2 NASU

[73] Romans 11:1; 2 Corinthians 11:22

David (Matthew 1:1,6,17)

Son of David

David, a famous king of Israel, lived about 800 years after Abraham, around 1000 B.C. Old Testament prophets predicted the Messiah would be "a son of David."[74] Biblical writers used the phrase "son of David" to refer to David's immediate children[75] or any of his distant descendants.[76] When referring to Jesus as "a son of David,"[77] Matthew did not imply David fathered Jesus directly, but that Jesus *descended* from David, His ancestor.[78]

"Son of David" also became a figure of speech synonymous with Messiah.[79] By referring to Jesus as "Son of David," Jews acknowledged His identity as the Christ, the Messiah – the Anointed One.[80]

A Man After God's Heart

You may recall the battle between David and the giant Goliath[81] or perhaps you remember David's shameful liaison with Bathsheba.[82] Though he had faults, David dedicated himself to serving God in whatever role he found himself, as a shepherd, warrior, musician, poet, and as king of Israel. David, one of God's prophets,[83] also composed almost half of the Old Testament book of Psalms.

---

[74] Acts 2:29-30; Psalm 89:3-4; Psalm 132:10-11; Micah 5:2
[75] 2 Samuel 13:1; 1 Chronicles 3:1,9; 1 Chronicles 29:22; 2 Chronicles 11:18; Luke 3:31
[76] Matthew 1:20
[77] Matthew 1:1 BT
[78] Matthew 1:1-17; Matthew documented Jesus' *legal* affiliation with David through his adoptive father Joseph, while Luke traced Jesus' *biological* affiliation with David through the family history of Mary, Jesus' mother (Luke 3:23-38). For a more detailed comparison of Matthew's genealogy of Jesus with that of Luke's record, see "Chapter 2 – Kings & Scoundrels: Jesus' Ancestors," heading "Jacob Fathered Joseph (Matthew 1:16)."
[79] Matthew 12:23; Matthew 22:42; Mark 12:35
[80] Matthew 15:22; Matthew 20:30-31; Matthew 21:9,15; Mark 10:47-48; Luke 18:38-39; For a discussion regarding the anointing of Jesus by the Father, see "Chapter 10 – Jesus Fulfills All Righteousness," heading "Spirit of God Descending (Matthew 3:16)."
[81] 1 Samuel 17:1-58
[82] 2 Samuel 11:1-27
[83] Acts 2:29-31

Extremely devoted to others, David remained loyal to his predecessor King Saul even when Saul, out of envy, tried to take David's life.[84] He shared a friendship closer than that of a blood relative with Jonathan, Saul's son.[85] Due to David's intense faith, God described him as, "A man after My heart, who will do all My will."[86] Who would not feel honored to have come from the family line of David? Even the Messiah chose birth as a "son of David."[87]

Sadly, the nation of Israel brought doom on itself by not continuing to follow David's godly example after he passed away.

***

<u>*Contemplation Point*</u>

- Could God describe you as a person after His heart?
  - If so, how so?
  - If not, what change in lifestyle would you need to make to fit that description?

---

[84] 1 Samuel 18:8-12; 1 Samuel 26:1-25
[85] 1 Samuel 18:1-5; 20:1-4
[86] Acts 13:22 NASU; 1 Samuel 13:13-15; 1 Kings 11:4
[87] Matthew 1:1 BT; Acts 2:29-30; Psalm 89:3-4; 132:10-11; Micah 5:2

The Babylonian Deportation (Matthew 1:11)

Civil War

In 922 B.C., about 900 years after Abraham arrived in Canaan and around 50 years after King David died, the nation of Israel divided into two kingdoms. Ten tribes broke away from the governing monarch to establish the *Kingdom of Israel*, sometimes referred to as the Northern Kingdom. Those ten tribes included Dan, Rueben, Ephraim, Gad, Manasseh, East Manasseh, Issachar, Naphtali, Zebulun, and Asher. The remaining tribes of Judah, Benjamin, Simeon, and Levi[88] formed the *Kingdom of Judah*, at times referred to as the Southern Kingdom. Shortly thereafter civil war erupted.

Assyrian Deportation (of Israel)

In 734 B.C., 188 years after the split of the Israelite nation, King Tiglath-pileser[89] of Assyria conquered the northern Kingdom of Israel.[90] He relocated a great number of the Israelites to Assyria, and on multiple occasions over the next 150 years the Assyrians deported thousands more. Details concerning those exiled Israelites beyond the time of their deportation remain uncertain.

Babylonian Deportation (of Judah)

Tiglath-pileser, the Assyrian king, chose not to occupy the southern Kingdom of Judah in lieu of Judah's offer to serve as his ally. Nonetheless, Judah paid tribute[91] to Assyria for the next 135 years to retain its nominal independence. Following the defeat of Assyria by King Nabopolassar of Babylonia in 612 B.C., Judah proceeded to pay tribute to

---

[88] 2 Chronicles 11:1,13; Joshua 19:9; The tribe of Levi remained loyal to King Rehoboam of Judah and God's Temple in Jerusalem.

[89] Historians identify the Assyrian king Tiglath-pileser as Tiglath-pileser III, sometimes spelled Tiglath-Pileser III.

[90] 2 Kings 15:29

[91] Tribute, a payment by a weaker nation to a stronger nation, demonstrated submission to the superior nation in exchange for the superior nation's promise not to invade.

Babylonia.

During the ensuing decades, the Kingdom of Judah became unfaithful to God. Assimilating the polytheistic[92] practices of neighboring nations, Judah chose to recognize and worship false gods, breaking its covenant[93] with the one and only God.[94] Consequently, the prophet Jeremiah rebuked the leaders of Judah, warning that God would allow them to fall to Babylonia if they did not change their ways.[95] Nevertheless, they continued to worship idols.[96]

The Kingdom of Judah rebelled against Babylonia, refusing to pay its customary tribute, which provoked Babylonia's 598 B.C. invasion. True to His word, God permitted the Babylonians to overthrow Judah. On March 16, 597 B.C., King Nebuchadnezzar[97] conquered Jerusalem.

Tens of thousands of Judahites became reluctant colonists in foreign lands as the Babylonians relocated them to various regions of the Babylonian Empire. Over the next several decades, the Babylonians deported Judahites on multiple occasions. Josiah (more precisely Josiah's son, Jehoiakim)[98] found himself caught up in one of those deportations, evident from the genealogy[99] listed by Matthew.[100] Following his deportation, Jehoiakim (Josiah's son) fathered Jechoniah.

In 539 B.C., King Cyrus the Great of the Persian Empire conquered Babylonia. As policy, Cyrus allowed exiled populations to return to their homelands once he defeated their conquerors. Thus Jechoniah returned to

---

[92] Judah came to practice polytheism, worship of more than one god.

[93] Two or more individuals establish a *covenant* when they create an agreement among themselves or declare a promise one to the other.

[94] John 17:3; John 5:44; 1 Timothy 1:17; Jude 25

[95] Jeremiah 13:19; 20:4; 25:2-11; 32:28

[96] An idol consists of an image that portrays a false god, often in the form of a statue.

[97] Nebuchadnezzar (něb-ü-khǎd-něz-zər)

[98] 1 Chronicles 3:14-17 lists Jechoniah as Jehoiakim's son and Josiah's grandson. Matthew's insertion of Josiah's name in place of Jehoiakim's name (Josiah's son) should cause no concern, for genealogical writers at times abridged ancestral lists by omitting names in this manner. For a discussion of omission of names in Israelite genealogies, see "Chapter 2 – Kings & Scoundrels: Jesus' Ancestors," heading "Jacob Fathered Joseph (Matthew 1:16)," subheading "Omission of Names."

[99] A genealogy lists ancestors in order of birth, sometimes in reverse order.

[100] Matthew 1:11

Judea and fathered Salathiel, an ancestor of Jesus.[101]

The Women (Matthew 1:3,5,6,16)

In his list of Jesus' ancestors, Matthew took the liberty of noting a handful of women, peculiar because Jews traced ancestry only through fathers. They never wrote females into the genealogical records. If a family ended its line with a daughter, the registrar would enter her husband's name in the official registry in her place as the son of her father.

The narrow-minded Jewish leaders of that day would have scoffed at Matthew's genealogy of Jesus due to his inclusion of women, especially these women.

- Matthew 1:3 – *Tamar* committed sexual immorality with her father-in-law, Judah.[102]
- Matthew 1:5 – *Rahab*, a Gentile,[103] at one time made her living as a prostitute in the city of Jericho.[104]
- Matthew 1:5 – *Ruth*, another Gentile, came from the nation of Moab.[105]
- Matthew 1:6 – *Bathsheba*, Uriah's wife, committed adultery with David.[106]
- Matthew 1:16 – *Mary*, Jesus' mother, became pregnant out of wedlock.

All Jewish households recognized the names and stories of Tamar, Rahab, Ruth, and Bathsheba, while Christians readily acknowledged the story of Mary. Yet, many unbelieving Jews would have scorned Jesus because those women played a part in His family history. So, why did Matthew include them?

Matthew subtly demonstrated that *no one* remains beyond God's

---

[101] Matthew 1:12
[102] Genesis 38:1-30
[103] The Jews identified a Gentile as anyone not of the bloodline of Jacob, son of Isaac, grandson of Abraham. God gave Jacob the name *Israel* (Genesis 32:28).
[104] Joshua 2:1-7
[105] Ruth 1:4
[106] 2 Samuel 11:1-4

gracious touch, regardless of ethnic origin or personal shortcomings. As the apostle Paul reminded the church in Galatia,

> *God shows no partiality.[107] ... There is neither **Jew nor Greek**, there is neither **slave nor free man**, there is neither **male nor female**; for you are all one in Christ Jesus. And if you belong to Christ, then you are Abraham's descendants, heirs according to promise.[108]*

***

Contemplation Points

1. Have you discriminated or shown favoritism based on superficial characteristics such as gender, race, wealth, popularity, or rank in society?
2. How do you manage to avoid such behavior?

Jacob Fathered Joseph (Matthew 1:16)

Scriptural Error?

Even though Matthew and Luke both traced Jesus' ancestry to Abraham,[109] at first reading their genealogical lists appear at odds. For instance, Matthew wrote, "Jacob fathered Joseph,"[110] while Luke called Joseph "the son of Eli."[111] Knowledge of the legal practice of that day helps to resolve the dilemma.

As discussed earlier, if a family ended its line with a daughter, the registrar would enter her husband's name into the registry in her place, listing him as the son of his wife's father. Luke traced Mary's lineage in that manner, conforming to the tradition of naming Joseph, Mary's husband, in her stead. Joseph, though biologically the son of Jacob, served

---

[107] Galatians 2:6 NASU; Romans 2:11; Acts 10:34-35
[108] Galatians 3:28-29 NASU
[109] Matthew 1:1-2; Luke 3:34
[110] Matthew 1:16 BT
[111] Luke 3:23 NASU; Some translators refer to Eli as "Heli."

as "the son of Eli" for legal purposes.[112]

Overlapping Family Lines

A review of Jesus' ancestry discloses that both Joseph[113] and Mary[114] descended from David. Hence, Jesus descended from David through the *biological* motherhood of Mary,[115] as well as the *legal* adoptive fatherhood of Joseph.[116]

The bloodlines of Joseph and Mary again intersected with Zerubbabel. Joseph descended through Abiud,[117] Zerubbabel's oldest son, and Mary descended through Zerubbabel's youngest son, Rhesa.[118]

Furthermore, Mary and Joseph had the same paternal grandfather, Matthan. Matthan, as Matthew called him,[119] or Matthat, as Luke referred to him,[120] fathered Jacob (Joseph's father) and Eli (Mary's father), making Mary and Joseph first cousins.[121]

Joseph & Mary: First Cousins

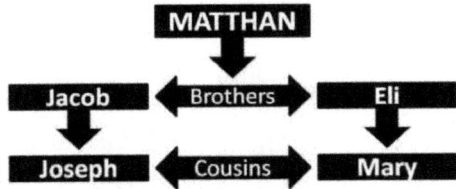

Figure 2 - 8

---

[112] Jews commonly omitted the *in-law* reference when discussing their family relationships. For example, consider the rapport between Naomi and her daughters-in-law, among them Ruth. Naomi affectionately referred to her daughters-in-law as her "daughters" (Ruth 1:11-13 NASU).

[113] Matthew 1:6

[114] Luke 3:31

[115] Romans 1:3; Luke 3:23-38 (Take special note of verses 23 and 31.)

[116] Matthew 1:1-17 (Take special note of verses 6 and 16.)

[117] Matthew 1:13

[118] Luke 3:27

[119] Matthew 1:15

[120] Luke 3:24

[121] Jewish civil law permitted first cousins to marry. God never prohibited such marriage in His Scriptures. For a list of intimate relationships forbidden by God for the Israelites, read Leviticus 18:5-24.

Fourteen Generations (Matthew 1:17)

Three Groups of 14

Matthew organized the generations of Jesus' ancestors into three groups of 14. Each group encompassed a major historical period of Israel's history.

- From Abraham to David
- From David to the Babylonian deportation
- From the Babylonian deportation to Jesus, the Messiah

Matthew designed a format more readily remembered by placing David as the last name of the first 14 and the first name of the second 14, then making the Babylonian deportation the last item of the second 14 and the first item of the third 14.

THREE GROUPS OF 14			
1	**ABRAHAM**	**DAVID** (& Uriah's wife)	**AFTER BABYLONIAN DEPORTATION** Jechoniah
2	Isaac	Solomon	Salathiel
3	Jacob	Rehoboam	Zerubbabel
4	Judah (& Tamar)	Abijah	Abiud
5	Perez	Asaph	Eliakim
6	Hezron	Jehoshaphat	Azor
7	Aram	Joram	Sadok
8	Aminadab	Uzziah	Achim
9	Nahshon	Jotham	Eliud
10	Salmon (& Rahab)	Ahaz	Eleazar
11	Boaz (& Ruth)	Hezekiah	Matthan
12	Obed	Manasseh	Jacob
13	Jesse	Amos	Joseph (& Mary)
14	**DAVID**	Josiah **DURING BABYLONIAN DEPORTATION**	**JESUS**

Omission of Names

Matthew adopted a practice utilized by some Old Testament prophets who skipped a generation here and there when recording a family line. At times, genealogical lists passed over generations, employing the phrase "a son of" in reference to a distant descendant, not an immediate descendant.[122] For instance, the genealogy of priests listed in Ezra 7:1-5 omits six names mentioned in a similar genealogy in 1 Chronicles 6:3-15. Matthew's abridged genealogy of Jesus should not create concern, for he did not omit names by error.

Likewise, the term "father" can refer to an immediate father or any male ancestor.[123] Consequently, when Matthew wrote "fathered," he applied the term to immediate fathers as well as forefathers.

Although we may prefer biblical authors to have written all-inclusive ancestral lists, the context[124] of the Jesus story concerns an early historical era and a society different from ours. The manner in which ancient Jews kept records met the purposes of *their* time and culture. Omission of certain names in a genealogy did not affect the legitimacy of ancestral history, nor did law require an exhaustive genealogical record as evidence for inheritance.

---

[122] Matthew 1:1

[123] Genesis 17:4-5; 19:37; 28:13; 32:9; Deuteronomy 1:11; 1 Kings 15:24; 22:50; 2 Kings 14:3; Isaiah 51:2; Matthew 3:9; Mark 11:10; Luke 1:32,73; 3:8; Matthew 3:24; John 8:39,53

[124] Context, the communication before and after a word or passage, often sheds light on the meaning intended by the writer or speaker.

Addition of Names

As discussed above, Matthew's omission of names should create no concern. Likewise, his addition of names absent from Old Testament genealogies should cause no apprehension. Keep in mind, Matthew did not write autonomously, for "all Scripture is inspired by God."[125] God, Himself, led Matthew[126] to trace Jesus' bloodline through individuals otherwise unknown.

Review of Matthew's Text (Matthew 1:1-17)

1 A book about the life of Jesus Christ, a son of David, a son of Abraham.

*2 **Abraham** fathered Isaac,*

***Isaac** fathered Jacob,*

***Jacob** fathered Judah and his brothers,*

*3 **Judah** fathered Perez and Zerah through **Tamar**,*

***Perez** fathered Hezron,*

***Hezron** fathered Aram, [127]*

*4 **Aram** fathered Aminadab,*

***Aminadab** fathered Nahshon,*

***Nahshon** fathered Salmon,*

*5 **Salmon** fathered Boaz through **Rahab**,*

***Boaz** fathered Obed through **Ruth**,*

***Obed** fathered Jesse,*

*6 **Jesse** fathered David the king.*

***David** fathered Solomon through **Uriah's wife**,[128]*

*7 **Solomon** fathered Rehoboam,*

***Rehoboam** fathered Abijah,*

***Abijah** fathered Asaph, [129]*

*8 **Asaph** fathered Jehoshaphat,*

---

125 2 Timothy 3:16 NASU
126 2 Peter 1:20-21; 2 Timothy 3:16
127 Some translators refer to Aram as "Ram."
128 Uriah's wife – Bathsheba
129 Some translators refer to Asaph as "Asa."

Jehoshaphat fathered Joram, [130]
Joram fathered Uzziah,
9 *Uzziah fathered Joatham, [131]*
Joatham fathered Ahaz,
Ahaz fathered Hezekiah,
10 *Hezekiah fathered Manasseh,*
Manasseh fathered Amos, [132]
Amos fathered Josiah,
11 *Josiah fathered Jechoniah and his brothers during the Babylonian deportation.*
12 *After the Babylonian deportation,*
Jechoniah fathered Salathiel,
Salathiel fathered Zerubbabel,
13 *Zerubbabel fathered Abiud,*
Abiud fathered Eliakim,
Eliakim fathered Azor,
14 *Azor fathered Sadok, [133]*
Sadok fathered Achim,
Achim fathered Eliud,
15 *Eliud fathered Eleazar,*
Eleazar fathered Matthan,
Matthan fathered Jacob,
16 *Jacob fathered Joseph, Mary's husband, through whom was born Jesus, the One called Christ.*
17 *Altogether there were fourteen generations from Abraham to David, and from David to the Babylonian deportation were fourteen generations, and from the Babylonian deportation to the Christ were fourteen generations.* (BT)[134]

---

[130] Some translators refer to Joram as "Jehoram."
[131] Some translators refer to Joatham as "Jotham."
[132] Some translators refer to Amos as "Amon."
[133] Some translators refer to Sadok as "Zadok."
[134] The abbreviation BT stands for Bagby Translation. For information concerning the Bagby Translation, see "Appendix 2: The Bagby Translation."

CHAPTER 3

....

Birth of Jesus, Rescuer of His People

Just as Jesus' family lineage aligned with that foretold about the Messiah by Old Testament prophets, the circumstances of His birth fulfilled prophecy as well. Though biologically impossible for Jesus' mother to have conceived without having had intimate relations with a man, the angel Gabriel confidently proclaimed to her, "Nothing will be impossible with God."[135] Thus the Father arranged the birth of "the only begotten God."[136]

---

[135] Luke 1:37 NASU
[136] John 1:18 NASU

Matthew's Text (Matthew 1:18-25)[137]

18 Now, the birth of Jesus Christ was as follows.

His mother Mary was engaged to Joseph. Before they came together, she was found to be pregnant through the Holy Spirit. 19 Joseph, her fiancé, being just and not wanting to expose her publicly, planned to separate from her privately.

20 Nonetheless, after he had reflected on these things, listen, an angel of the Lord appeared to him through a dream, saying, "Joseph, son of David, do not be afraid to accept Mary as your fiancée, because that which is in her has been created through the Holy Spirit. 21 She will give birth to a Son, and you will call His name Jesus, for He, Himself, will rescue His people from their sins."

22 Now, all this has taken place so that which had been spoken by the Lord through the prophet might be fulfilled, saying, 23 "Behold, a virgin will conceive and give birth to a Son, and they will call His name Emmanuel," which translated means "God with us."

24 Having roused from his sleep, Joseph did as the angel of the Lord had commanded him. After that, he accepted his fiancée 25 and had no sexual relations with her until after she gave birth to a Son. Then he called His name Jesus. (BT)

---

[137] No passages within the books of Mark, Luke, or John parallel Matthew 1:18-25.

Mary (Matthew 1:18)

The Favored One

Gabriel startled Mary when he declared, "Greetings, favored one! ... You have found favor with God."[138] *Kecharitoméne* (kĕ-khär-ĭ-tō-mĕ́-nā),[139] the Greek word translated "favored one," describes a person shown *unmerited* kindness. The Father did not choose Mary as the Messiah's mother because she deserved it.

On a later occasion, following Mary's greeting to her relative, Elizabeth, "Elizabeth ... filled with the Holy Spirit ... cried out ..., 'Blessed are you among women.'"[140] *Eulogaméne* (ĕü-lŏ-gä-mĕ́-nā),[141] the Greek word translated "blessed," means literally "having been well spoken of." However, it does not imply the person spoken well of merited preferential treatment.

Shortly after Elizabeth's statement, Mary commented, "From this time on all generations will count me blessed. For the Mighty One has done great things for me."[142] *Makariousín* (mä-kä-rĭ-ŏü-sĭ́n),[143] the Greek word translated "will count blessed" means literally "will call fortunate." The word describes someone who received the benefit of another person's benevolent action, but does not imply the fortunate individual merited special privilege.

Although the Father could have selected any woman as the mother of His Son, He led His prophets to foretell that a virgin would give birth to the Messiah,[144] a woman who would descend from King David.[145] Mary fulfilled both conditions. The Scriptures do not indicate Mary deserved the Father's choice of her over other righteous virgin descendants of David.

---

[138] Luke 1:28 NASU

[139] *Kecharitoméne* (kĕ-khär-ĭ-tō-mĕ́-nā), κεχαριτωμένη

[140] Luke 1:41-42 NASU

[141] *Eulogaméne* (ĕü-lŏ-gä-mĕ́-nā), εὐλογημένη

[142] Luke 1:48-49 NASU

[143] *Makariousín* (mä-kä-rĭ-ŏü-sĭ́n), μακαριοῦσίν

[144] Isaiah 7:14

[145] Acts 2:29-30; Psalm 89:3-4; 132:10-11; Micah 5:2

She did nothing great to warrant the Father's favor. To the contrary, Mary clarified, "the Mighty One has done great things for *me*."[146]

Submissive Character

"Greetings, favored one! The Lord is with you."[147]

As quickly as Mary heard the salutation, she caught sight of an angel "coming in."[148] Gabriel's abrupt appearance would have overwhelmed her.

He announced, "You will conceive in your womb and bear a son, and you shall name Him Jesus."[149]

Hesitating, she asked, "How can this be, since I am a virgin?"[150]

He answered, "The Holy Spirit will come upon you, and the power of the Most High will overshadow you; and for that reason the holy Child shall be called the Son of God."[151]

Gabriel's statements left Mary perplexed. Even so, she bowed to God's will, replying, "Behold, the bondslave of the Lord; may it be done to me according to your word."[152]

Some thirty years later, Mary's divine Son submitted Himself to God the Father, continuing His life-long practice.[153] Facing death on a Roman cross, Jesus followed His mother's example. In complete surrender, He avowed, "Not as I wish, but as You desire."[154] God the Father chose His Son's mother well.

---

[146] Luke 1:48-49 NASU
[147] Luke 1:28 NASU
[148] Luke 1:28 NASU
[149] Luke 1:31 NASU
[150] Luke 1:34 NASU
[151] Luke 1:35 NASU
[152] Luke 1:38 NASU
[153] John 6:38 BT; Matthew 26:39; Mark 14:36; Luke 22:42
[154] Matthew 26:39 BT

***

Contemplation Points

1. Have you surrendered your life to the will of God?
2. How have you submitted to *God's* desires in lieu of doing what *you* would otherwise choose?

Unassuming Character

Mary never drew attention to herself as the mother of Jesus. His four biographers (Matthew, Mark, Luke, and John) rarely mentioned her in their stories after telling of her giving birth to Jesus. The Scriptures refer to Mary on only four occasions after Jesus' departure from His family's home in Nazareth.

- A wedding in the town of Cana[155]
- Outside a house in the city of Capernaum, waiting in a crowd to speak with Jesus[156]
- The crucifixion of Jesus[157]
- Engaged in prayer with other Christians in Jerusalem[158]

After Jesus' crucifixion, Mary likely remained in Jerusalem in the care of Jesus' apostle John for the remainder of her life.[159]

***

Contemplation Point

- If God chooses you to accomplish a special purpose on His behalf, how will you manage to maintain an unassuming character as Mary did?

---

[155] John 2:1-5
[156] Matthew 12:46; John 2:12
[157] John 19:25-27
[158] Acts 1:14
[159] John 19:26-27

Daring Character

After Gabriel informed Mary she would conceive a child through the Holy Spirit,[160] he further advised her that Elizabeth, her elderly relative,[161] had also conceived a son.[162] Mary "went in a hurry" to visit Elizabeth.[163] She faced a strenuous journey, for Elizabeth lived far south of Nazareth, in a city within the hill country of Judea.[164]

Zacharias, Elizabeth's husband, served as a priest.[165] All priests of Israel were Levites,[166] specifically of Aaron's family line.[167] Eight of the 48 cities[168] God gave the tribe of Levi lay within the hill country of Judea. The eight cities were Hebron, Libnah, Jattir, Eshtemoa, Holon,[169] Debir, Juttah, and Beth-shemesh.[170] Although Luke never mentioned the name of the city in which Elizabeth lived, she and Zacharias would have resided in one of those eight towns.

Hebron, one of the eight, developed into the chief city within the hill country of Judea and will function as our reference point to calculate the approximate distance Mary traveled to visit Elizabeth. The city lay about 19 miles[171] south of Jerusalem, in a shallow valley west of the Dead Sea. Mary would have traveled southward from Nazareth at least 82 miles[172] before reaching Hebron, depending on the route she took. Traversing that distance required a journey of over a week.

---

[160] Luke 1:31-35

[161] Luke 1:36; The Greek word *sunggenís* (sŭng-gĕn-ís), συγγενίς, used by the angel in Luke 1:36 to refer to Elizabeth's relationship to Mary, means "female blood-relative," not cousin or aunt. The Scriptures never clarify the family relationship between Mary and Elizabeth.

[162] Luke 1:36-40

[163] Luke 1:39 NASU

[164] Luke 1:39

[165] Luke 1:5

[166] Levites, descendants of Levi but not of Aaron's bloodline, served as assistants to the priests, Levites of Aaron's bloodline. Under the direction of the priests, the non-priest Levites cared for the mundane needs of God's Temple (See 1 Chronicles 6:48; 23:3-6,26-32). For additional information regarding Levites, see "Appendix 3: Glossary."

[167] Aaron, the brother of Moses, served as Israel's first high priest.

[168] Joshua 21:1-42

[169] Holon, also known as Hilen (1 Chronicles 6:58)

[170] Joshua 21:4,9-16

[171] 30 kilometers

[172] 132 kilometers

Map: Nazareth to Hebron

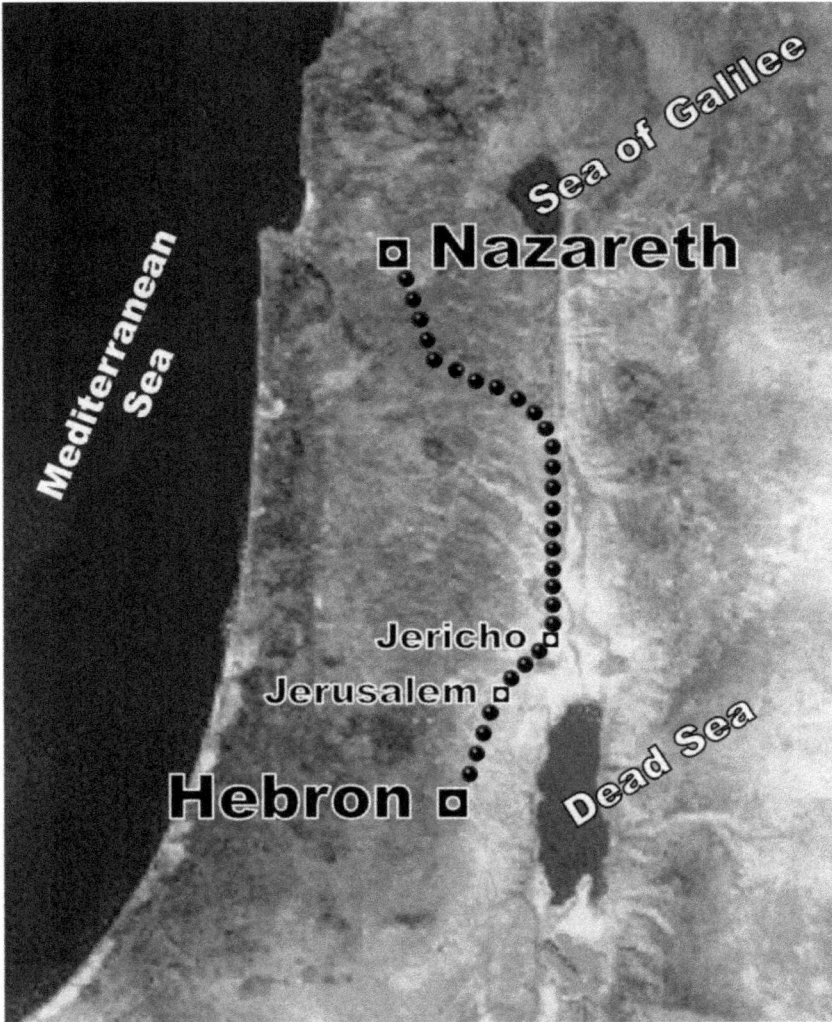

Figure 3 - 1

Hebron (About 1898 A.D.)

Figure 3 - 2

Hebron (About 1898 A.D.)

Figure 3 - 3

Hebron (About 1898 A.D.)

Figure 3 - 4

Mary, a young woman of daring character, chose to make the long journey to Judea without her fiancé. The Scriptures do not suggest anyone accompanied her, although a parting caravan could have prompted her quick departure. By whatever manner Mary traveled to Elizabeth's home, to initiate such an expedition demonstrated her adventurous spirit.

While both Elizabeth and her husband Zacharias had grown elderly, Mary remained comparatively young.[173] In spite of Elizabeth's advanced age, her pregnancy had progressed more than six months by the time Mary arrived.[174] Mary stayed three months,[175] long enough to allow her to help Elizabeth through the delivery of her baby.

---

[173] Luke 1:7
[174] Luke 1:35-40
[175] Luke 1:56

Zacharias named his son John, as instructed by an angel over six months earlier.[176] John served as a prophet of God after he grew up.[177] The public referred to him as *John the Immerser*.[178]

Joseph (Matthew 1:18)

Joseph the Craftsman

Joseph worked as a craftsman. Customarily, he would have trained Jesus to follow the same vocation[179] and likely prepared Jesus' brothers[180] to work in the family business as well.

The majority of translators utilize the word "carpenter" to convey the occupation of Joseph. *Xulourgós* (zü-lŏür-gŏs),[181] the Greek word properly translated carpenter, literally means "wood worker." Yet, no writer used *xulourgós* anywhere in the New Testament.

Matthew employed the Greek word *téktonos* (tĕk-tŏn-ŏs)[182] to describe Joseph's trade. *Téktonos* forms the genitive[183] case of the Greek noun *tékton* (tĕk-tōn),[184] which means "craftsman." Bystanders in Nazareth identified Jesus as a *tékton* (craftsman),[185] not a *xulourgós* (wood worker).

The work performed by a *tékton* (craftsman) could involve stone, wood, metal, or any combination of those materials, depending on the

---

[176] Luke 1:13

[177] Luke 7:24-26

[178] Immerser – *Baptistés* (Băp-tĭs-tăs, βαπτιστὴς), the Greek word translated "Immerser," often finds itself *transliterated* as "Baptist," instead of *translated* precisely as "Immerser." For more information about John, see "Chapter 8 – The Desert Prophet." For a discussion of the origin of the word "Baptist," see "Chapter 8 – The Desert Prophet," heading "They Were Immersed (Matthew 3:6)."

[179] Matthew 13:55; Mark 6:3

[180] Matthew 12:46-47; 13:55-56; Mark 3:31-32; Luke 8:19-20; John 7:3-5,10

[181] *Xulourgós* (zü-lŏür-gŏs), ξύλυοργός

[182] *Téktonos* (tĕk-tŏn-ŏs), τέκτονος; Matthew 13:55

[183] The Greek grammatical genitive case denotes possession, or a relation similar to possession, as in "the son *of* the craftsman" (Matthew 13:55 BT).

[184] *Tékton* (tĕk-tōn), τέκτων

[185] "Is this not the *craftsman*" (Mark 6:3 BT).

context[186] in which a writer employed the word. Luke referred to the silversmiths in Ephesus as craftsmen,[187] calling them *teknítais* (tĕk-nĭ́-täĭs),[188] the plural of *teknítas* (tĕk-nĭ́-tās),[189] a close synonym of *tékton*. Since no biblical text mentions the exact material with which Joseph or Jesus worked, anyone who identifies them as carpenters has done so based on legend. Instead, consider the environmental and cultural contexts of their day.

In ancient Judea, a *tékton* (craftsman) utilized stone to fabricate buildings,[190] city walls,[191] houses,[192] animal troughs,[193] water pots,[194] millstones,[195] and numerous other commodities.[196] They found stone readily available and inexpensive, while craft-quality wood remained a rare and expensive material. Considering these facts, Joseph and Jesus probably worked as common stone craftsmen, not as prosperous wood craftsmen skilled in fine artistic design.[197]

---

[186] Context, the communication before and after a word or passage, often sheds light on the meaning intended by the writer or speaker.

[187] Acts 19:24

[188] *Teknítais* (tĕk-nĭ́-täĭs), τεχνίταις

[189] *Teknítes* (tĕk-nĭ́-tās), τεχνίτης

[190] Mark 13:1-2; Luke 21:5-6

[191] Luke 19:43-44

[192] 1 Peter 2:4-5

[193] Luke 2:7,12,16; Ancient writers of English, 14th century A.D. and later, referred to an animal trough as a manger. For additional information regarding the animal troughs of ancient Israel, see "Chapter 5 – The Magi Meet Jesus, King of the Jews," heading "The Star Stood Above Where the Child Was (Matthew 2:9)."

[194] John 2:6

[195] Matthew 18:6; Mark 9:42; Luke 17:2

[196] Matthew 27:60

[197] Joseph did not make a living as a wealthy craftsman. For more information regarding his financial resources, see "Chapter 4 – The Magi Meet Herod, King of Judea," heading "His Star (Matthew 2:2)," subheading "When Did the Magi Arrive in Bethlehem?," subheading "Six-Week Time-Period."

Jerusalem Stone Craftsmen (About 1890 A.D.)

Figure 3 - 5

Jerusalem Stone Craftsman (About 1900 A.D.)

Figure 3 - 6

5 5 5 5

Joseph's Fate

History does not disclose how or when Joseph passed away. Luke's book contains the last recorded activity of Joseph's life, when he took Mary and twelve-year-old Jesus to attend the annual Passover celebration in Jerusalem.[198] In all probability, Mary's lack of a husband led Jesus, in the midst of His crucifixion, to commit His mother to the care of His trusted friend John, His apostle.[199] Joseph must have died sometime between Jesus' twelfth birthday and His crucifixion.

Mary Was Engaged to Joseph (Matthew 1:18)

Destined to become companions for life, Joseph and Mary would have come to know each other well as cousins[200] growing up in the small town of Nazareth.[201] Although the Scriptures do not specify the age of Mary or Joseph when they betrothed,[202] such marriage engagements typically took place when about eighteen years old.[203] Ten or twelve months usually passed between the time a couple officially promised themselves to one another and the wedding celebration.[204] Meanwhile, Mary would have lived with her parents in anticipation of the appointed day Joseph would take her to his own home as his wife.

The legal ramifications of a marriage engagement among the ancient Jews differed from those of our society. Once engaged, the betrothal legally bound both parties, even though they would not

---

[198] Luke 2:41-51; Also, see "Appendix 1: 12-Year-Old Jesus in Temple."

[199] John 19:27

[200] For Jewish civil law permitted first cousins to marry. God never prohibited such marriage in His Scriptures. For a list of intimate relationships forbidden by God for the Israelites, read Leviticus 18:5-24. For additional information regarding the family relationship of Joseph and Mary, see "Chapter 2 – Kings & Scoundrels: Jesus' Ancestors," heading "Jacob Fathered Joseph (Matthew 1:16)," subheading "Overlapping Family Lines."

[201] Luke 1:26-27; 2:4-5

[202] A betrothal refers to a marriage engagement.

[203] *New Edition of the Babylonian Talmud*, Volume 1, Translated by Michael Rodkinson, New Talmud Publishing Company, 100 Boylston St., Boston, MA, USA, (1896, p. 133, Tract Aboth, Tosephtha-Aboth of R. Nathan, Mishna EE)

[204] Genesis 24:55; Deuteronomy 20:7; Judges 14:7-8

consummate the marriage until the wedding day. Conditions of the pledge demanded that the woman's possessions immediately become the legal property of the husband-to-be, a type of guarantee and dowry. Moreover, cancellation of a marriage engagement required a formal, legal divorce.

Joseph Planned to Separate from Her (Matthew 1:19)

Upon returning to Nazareth from her visit with Elizabeth,[205] Mary would have shown physical signs of pregnancy as she entered her second trimester, a first opportunity for Joseph to notice her condition. Agonizing as he discovered his fiancée apparently had intimate relations with another man, Mary's explanation must have sounded ridiculous to him. Angered, grieved, and humiliated, Joseph contemplated how to proceed.

Termination of a betrothal required a legal divorce and Hebrew law classified sexual breach of a marriage engagement as adultery, punishable by death through stoning.[206] In spite of the situation, Joseph still cared for Mary's welfare. He planned to end their relationship discreetly instead of making a public example of her, which demonstrated his kind and sensitive spirit.

Joseph's righteous disposition stands out against the hypocritical actions of Judah, which appear in the Old Testament book of Genesis.[207] Judah found his widowed daughter-in-law, Tamar, pregnant but unmarried. Unlike Joseph, Judah promptly pronounced the severest punishment upon Tamar, unaware that he, himself, had fathered her child in a bizarre twist of events.

***

Contemplation Points

1. If challenged by a circumstance as difficult as Joseph's concerning Mary's pregnancy, would you respond with the love and sensitivity he showed her?
2. What actions would you take?

---

[205] Luke 1:5-56
[206] Deuteronomy 22:23-24
[207] Genesis 38:1-26

An Angel Appeared (Matthew 1:20)

After Joseph decided to end his marriage commitment, God sent an angel to intervene. Through a dream, the angel confirmed to Joseph, "That which is in her has been created through the Holy Spirit."[208]

The Greek word translated "angel" in the New Testament, *ánggelos* (áng-gĕ-lŏs),[209] means "messenger." The Hebrew word translated "angel" in the Old Testament, *málok* (mắl-ôk),[210] also means "messenger." In the course of everyday life, these words referred to anyone who delivered any communication on behalf of someone else.

God created thousands of angels, His personal messengers who reside in Heaven.[211] As spirit beings,[212] they have neither male nor female gender,[213] but do possess greater abilities than human beings.[214]

Throughout history, God sent angels to Earth to carry out special assignments. He occasionally deployed angels to destroy those who did not obey Him. For example, He dispatched two angels to destroy the evil cities of Sodom and Gomorrah.[215]

On the other hand, many of the tasks God assigned His angels involved aiding people who remained faithful to Him.[216] For instance, He sent an angel to protect the city of Jerusalem from the Assyrian army. That particular angel carried out his task with a preemptive strike, slaying 185,000 Assyrian soldiers in the middle of the night.[217]

However, God most often dispatched angels simply to communicate a message, as with Mary and Joseph.

---

[208] Matthew 1:20 BT
[209] *Ánggelos* (áng-gĕ-lŏs), ἄγγελος
[210] *Málok* (mắl-ôk), מלאך
[211] Psalm 148:1-5
[212] Hebrews 1:13-14
[213] Matthew 22:30
[214] Psalm 103:20; Hebrews 2:6-7; 2 Peter 2:9-11
[215] Genesis 19:12-29
[216] Genesis 24:40; Psalm 78:40-51; 91:10-11; Daniel 6:21-22; Acts 5:18-20; 12:5-8; Hebrews 1:13-14
[217] 2 Kings 19:31-36

Of the Lord (Matthew 1:20)

Matthew portrayed the angel who spoke to Joseph as one "of the Lord." *Kuríou* (kür-ḗ-ŏŭ),[218] the Greek word translated "of the Lord," forms the genitive[219] case of the Greek word *kúrios* (kŭr-ē-ŏs).[220] *Kúrios* described a person who had absolute authority over something or someone he possessed. Speakers of Greek frequently used *kúrios* in reference to the owner of slaves.

Depending on the context in which a writer employed *kúrios*, it could mean sir, ruler, owner, or master. However, when applied to Deity,[221] translators most often utilize the word "Lord." Among God's relationships with us are Ruler, Owner, Master, and Lord.

***

Contemplation Points

1. Are you "of the Lord?"
2. If so, how does your behavior reflect on God as your Ruler? Owner? Master? Lord?

Call His Name Jesus (Matthew 1:21)

Origin of the Name "Jesus"

The name *Jesus* came to English through Latin. Jerome,[222] in his 405 A.D. Latin Vulgate translation of the Scriptures, spelled our Savior's name *I-e-s-u-s* (yā-sŭs), a Latin transliteration[223] of the Greek name *Iesoús* (yā-sŏŭs),[224] itself a Greek transliteration of the Aramaic name *Yeshúa*

---

[218] *Kuríou* (kür-ḗ-ŏŭ), κυρίου

[219] The Greek grammatical genitive case denotes possession, or a relation similar to possession, as in "the son *of* the craftsman" (Matthew 13:55 BT).

[220] *Kúrios* (kŭr-ē-ŏs), κύριος

[221] The word deity means god.

[222] Jerome served as a Roman Catholic priest.

[223] When transliterating, instead of translating a word, a translator *spells out* an approximation of the original language's *pronunciation* of the word using the alphabet of the second language. For more details regarding transliteration, see "Appendix 3: Glossary."

[224] *Iesoús* (yā-sŏŭs), Ἰησοῦς

(yĕh-shŭä).[225] Not until 1592 A.D. did the Clementine Vulgate translation introduce the *J-e-s-ú-s* (yā-sús) spelling in its Latin revision of Jerome's work.[226]

The Jews Spoke Aramaic

Jews living in Judea spoke Aramaic at the time the angel delivered God's messages to Mary and Joseph. Several events produced that puzzling piece of history.

Aramaic, a Semitic (i.e., Shemitic) language closely related to Hebrew, emerged around 2000 B.C. through descendants of Aram, a son of Shem, Noah's oldest son.[227] Hebrew, also a Semitic language, developed through descendants of Eber,[228] a great-grandson of Shem and great-nephew of Aram.[229]

By the era of the Assyrian Empire (911-612 B.C.), merchants and diplomats throughout southwest Asia spoke Aramaic as their preferred professional language. Following Babylonia's conquest of Assyria,[230] Aramaic became one of the official languages of the Babylonian Empire (612-539 B.C.).

During the Babylonian deportation,[231] the exiles from the Kingdom of Judah began to speak Aramaic, blending Hebrew into their Aramaic speech. As a result, a Hebrew dialect[232] of Aramaic developed. Hebrew and Aramaic shared alphabetic characters and contained similar vocabulary, which facilitated the evolution of the new dialect.

---

[225] *Yeshúa* (yĕh-shŭä), יֵשׁוּעַ

[226] The Clementine Vulgate of 1592 A.D. revised Jerome's 405 A.D. Latin Vulgate translation and became the standard Bible text of the Roman Catholic Church until 1979 A.D., when the Nova Vulgata replaced it.

[227] Genesis 5:32; 10:22

[228] Eber, sometimes spelled "Heber"

[229] Genesis 10:21,24-25,31

[230] For additional information regarding Babylonia's conquest of Assyria, see "Chapter 2 – Kings & Scoundrels: Jesus' Ancestors," heading "The Babylonian Deportation (Matthew 1:11)."

[231] For additional information regarding the Babylonian deportation, see "Chapter 2 – Kings & Scoundrels: Jesus' Ancestors," heading "The Babylonian Deportation (Matthew 1:11)."

[232] Dialect – a regional style of spoken language distinguished by distinctive pronunciation, vocabulary, grammar, or any combination of the three characteristics

After the deportees returned from Babylonian exile to their Judean homeland (538 B.C.), they retained their distinct Hebrew dialect of Aramaic. Centuries later, during the Roman occupation of Judea, Jews continued to speak Aramaic as their first language. Hence, Mary and Joseph would have conversed daily in Aramaic.

Rescuer of His People

"You will call His name Jesus, for He, Himself, will *rescue* His people from their sins,"[233] the angel directed Joseph.

Since Joseph and Mary communicated in Aramaic day-to-day, the angel would have directed Joseph to call the Child by the Aramaic name *Yeshúa* (yĕh-shúä),[234] a diminutive[235] of the Hebrew name *Yehoshúa* (yĕh-hŏ-shúä).[236] The rationale for God's choice of the Aramaic name *Yeshúa* lies within the Hebrew language. In Hebrew, *Yehoshúa* means "*Yáhweh* rescues."[237] Accordingly, the angel declared to Joseph that God named His Son *Yeshúa*, "For He, Himself, will *rescue* His people from their sins."[238]

***

Contemplation Points

1. Have you ever found yourself in a hopeless situation in need of rescue?
2. If so, what emotions did you feel?
3. What actions did you take in hope of finding rescue?
4. What bond do you now feel toward your rescuer?
5. How strong a bond exists between you and Jesus, your spiritual Rescuer?

---

[233] Matthew 1:21 BT

[234] *Yeshúa* (yĕh-shúä), ישוע

[235] Diminutive – a shortened or altered form of a name

[236] *Yehoshúa* (yĕh-hŏ-shúä), יהושע; In the Old Testament, a man named *Yehoshúa* led the Israelites across the Jordan River into the promised land of Canaan.[236] Translators typically render his name as Joshua.

[237] In Exodus 6:3, God called Himself by the name *Yáhweh* (yáh-wĕh, יהוה), which means "the Existing One." Some translators weakly transliterate this Hebrew word as *Jehovah* instead of *Yáhweh*.

[238] Matthew 1:21 BT

A Virgin Will Conceive (Matthew 1:23)

"The Lord Himself will give you a sign," the prophet Isaiah wrote about seven centuries earlier, "A virgin will be with child and bear a Son."[239] Matthew presented Isaiah's statement as proof that God had arranged the birth of Jesus.

"How can this be, since I am a virgin?"[240] Mary responded, bewildered after Gabriel announced to her she would conceive a Son.

Gabriel answered straight to the point, explaining, "*Nothing* will be impossible with God."[241]

***

Contemplation Points

- When Gabriel explained to Mary, "Nothing will be impossible with God," what did he imply?
  - o Do you live as though you believe that implication?
  - o If so, how have you demonstrated your conviction?

They Will Call His Name Emmanuel (Matthew 1:23)

"They will call His name *Emmanuel*,"[242] Matthew cites from Isaiah. Yet, two verses earlier Matthew had the angel telling Joseph, "You will call His name *Jesus*."[243] Did Matthew contradict himself?

No, the Scriptures disclose several names related to Jesus. Joseph "called His name Jesus,"[244] exactly as the angel had instructed. However, Jesus' followers utilized additional names related to His nature and character.

---

[239] Isaiah 7:14 NASU; Matthew 1:23
[240] Luke 1:34 NASU
[241] Luke 1:37 NASU
[242] Matthew 1:23 BT; Isaiah 7:14
[243] Matthew 1:21 BT
[244] Matthew 1:25 BT

When conceding the absolute authority of Jesus, His disciples[245] called Him *Lord*,[246] a translation of the Greek word *kúrios*.[247] When acknowledging Jesus' status as the Anointed One,[248] His disciples spoke of Him as *Christ*,[249] a transliteration of the Greek word *Christós*.[250]

Pointing out Jesus' deity, Matthew drew attention to Isaiah's reference to Him as *Emmanuel*, an English transliteration of the Greek name *Emmanuál* (ĕm-mä-nü-ál),[251] itself a transliteration of the Hebrew name *Imanuél* (ĭm-ā́-nü-él),[252] which means "God with us." The apostle John described Jesus similarly as "the only begotten God,"[253] Deity born into a human body.

---

[245] The term *disciple* means "learner" and referred to believers who followed the teachings of Jesus. Sometimes the word described those who followed John the Immerser's teachings concerning Jesus (Matthew 9:14). Other times, the context of the word indicates a reference specifically to Jesus' apostles (Matthew 15:12-14).

[246] Matthew 14:30

[247] For information regarding the Greek word *kúrios*, see "Chapter 3 – Birth of Jesus, Rescuer of His People," heading "Of the Lord (Matthew 1:20)."

[248] For a discussion of the anointing of Jesus by the Father, see "Chapter 10 – Jesus Fulfills All Righteousness," heading "Spirit of God Descending (Matthew 3:16)."

[249] Matthew 11:2-5

[250] For information about the Greek word *Christós*, see "Chapter 2 – Kings & Scoundrels: Jesus' Ancestors," heading "Christ (Matthew 1:1)."

[251] Emmanuál (ĕm-mä-nü-ál), Ἐμμανουήλ

[252] Imanuél (ĭm-ā-nü-él), עמנואל

[253] John 1:18 NASU

Joseph Did as Commanded (Matthew 1:24-25)

Complex circumstances challenge wisdom, strain relationships, stir emotions erratically, and put faith to the test. Yet, Joseph's faith endured. He obeyed God and accepted Mary as his fiancée,[254] exactly as instructed.

***

Contemplation Points

1. What emotions might Joseph have felt during his ordeal?
2. How great a challenge did Joseph face to obey God in this matter? Explain.
3. Which of the following statements would have come closest to reflecting yours had you found yourself in Joseph's situation? Explain why.
    a. "God, why did You put me in this embarrassing position?"
    b. "God, thank You for choosing me."
4. How will you manage to trust and obey God when
    a. Life's circumstances become confusing and hard to handle?
    b. Peer pressure challenges your obedience?
5. In Joseph's place, how would you have explained the situation to your family and friends?

---

[254] Joseph "did as the angel of the Lord had commanded" and accepted Mary as his *fiancée*, instead of separating from her as he had planned (Matthew 1:24 BT). They did not become husband and wife at that time, for Luke notes they remained "engaged" sometime later when they departed for Bethlehem (Luke 2:4-5 NASU).

No Sexual Relations Until After Birth (Matthew 1:25)

Even though Joseph abandoned his plan to separate from Mary, he "had no sexual relations with her *until after* she gave birth."[255] The words "until after" imply Joseph and Mary later carried out their intimate marital responsibility to each other. They fulfilled God's interactive design for married couples. As the apostle Paul instructed the spouses within the Corinthian church,

> *The husband must fulfill his duty to his wife, and likewise also the wife to her husband. The wife does not have authority over her own body, but the husband does; and likewise also the husband does not have authority over his own body, but the wife does. Stop depriving one another, except by agreement for a time, so that you may devote yourselves to prayer, and come together again so that Satan will not tempt you because of your lack of self-control.*[256]

Scriptural references to Jesus' siblings further indicate Joseph and Mary did not remain celibate following His birth.[257]

[255] Matthew 1:25 BT
[256] 1 Corinthians 7:3-5 NASU
[257] Matthew 13:55-56; 12:46-47; Mark 3:31-32; Luke 8:19-20; John 7:3-5,10

Review of Matthew's Text (Matthew 1:18-25)

18 Now, the birth of Jesus Christ was as follows.

His mother Mary was engaged to Joseph. Before they came together, she was found to be pregnant through the Holy Spirit. 19 Joseph, her fiancé, being just and not wanting to expose her publicly, planned to separate from her privately.

20 Nonetheless, after he had reflected on these things, listen, an angel of the Lord appeared to him through a dream, saying, "Joseph, son of David, do not be afraid to accept Mary as your fiancée, because that which is in her has been created through the Holy Spirit. 21 She will give birth to a Son, and you will call His name Jesus, for He, Himself, will rescue His people from their sins."

22 Now, all this has taken place so that which had been spoken by the Lord through the prophet might be fulfilled, saying, 23 "Behold, a virgin will conceive and give birth to a Son, and they will call His name Emmanuel," which translated means "God with us."

24 Having roused from his sleep, Joseph did as the angel of the Lord had commanded him. After that, he accepted his fiancée 25 and had no sexual relations with her until after she gave birth to a Son. Then he called His name Jesus. (BT)

CHAPTER 4

....

The Magi Meet Herod, King of Judea

After nearly a century of civil wars, the Roman Senate appointed Gaius Julius Caesar Octavianus[258] as the first emperor of the Roman Empire and gave him the title Augustus[259] Princeps.[260] Augustus, who ruled from 27 B.C. until his death in 14 A.D., restored unity to the empire and created an orderly government. Historians refer to that era as the *Augustan Age*.

The Augustan Age brought a time of relative peace and prosperity within most of the territories of the Roman Empire. Nevertheless, Roman Judea suffered exceptional unrest under its corrupt and ruthless king, Herod.

While Joseph and Mary planned their new life together, Augustus planned their taxation. He decreed that Roman officials take a census of

---

[258] Citizens of the Roman Empire came to address all Roman emperors by the title *Caesar*.
[259] Augustus – Latin "illustrious one"
[260] Princeps – Latin "first"

the Roman Empire to hold all inhabitants accountable for payment of taxes due.[261] Since Jews maintained family genealogical records in their ancestral towns, all individuals journeyed to the home of their principal ancestor to register in the census. Joseph and Mary, both descendants of King David, traveled to David's hometown of Bethlehem.

Following their arrival in Bethlehem, Mary gave birth to Jesus. Sometime after Jesus' birth, Magi[262] from a land far northeast of Judea arrived in Jerusalem searching for "the One who has been born King of the Jews."[263]

Matthew's Text (Matthew 2:1-8)[264]

1 In the days of King Herod, after Jesus was born in Bethlehem of Judea, listen now, Magi from the East arrived in Jerusalem, 2 saying, "Where is the One who has been born King of the Jews? We saw His star in the east and we came to worship Him."

3 Having heard this, King Herod was troubled and all Jerusalem with him. 4 Then, bringing together all the chief priests and scribes of the people, he was asking them where the Christ was to be born.

5 They said to him, "In Bethlehem of Judah, for it has been written through the prophet, 6 'And you Bethlehem of the land of Judah, you are not at all least among the leaders of Judah; for from you will come forth a Leader who will shepherd My people, Israel.'"

7 Then Herod, having called the Magi privately, learned from them the precise time of the appearance of the star.

8 Later, sending them to Bethlehem, he said, "When you[265] get there, make detailed inquiries about the Child. Tell me when

---

[261] Luke 2:1-5

[262] "Magi" forms the plural of magus. For more information about the Magi, see "Chapter 4 – The Magi Meet Herod, King of Judea," heading "Magi from the East (Matthew 2:1)."

[263] Matthew 2:2 BT

[264] No passages within the books of Mark, Luke, or John parallel Matthew 2:1-8.

[265] To convey the intent of Matthew's Greek text, the BT marks *you* and *your* with a double underscore when plural (i.e., you, your).

you find Him, so that I might also come to worship Him." (BT)

King Herod the Great (Matthew 2:1)

Politics

Historians refer to King Herod by the illustrious name *Herod the Great*. Before becoming Rome's client-king[266] of Judea, Herod diligently sought the favor of Mark Antony, who ruled the Roman Empire 43-33 B.C. in a triumvirate[267] together with Lepidus and Octavian.

In 40 B.C., the Roman Senate gave Mark Antony responsibility for the eastern portion of the Roman Empire. His territory extended from the Adriatic Sea in the west to the Euphrates River in the east. To Herod's delight, Judea lay within Antony's new jurisdiction.

Having successfully obtained the political support of Mark Antony, Herod received the title *King of the Jews* from the Roman Senate in 39 B.C. Yet, due to political turmoil in Judea, he did not effectively exercise control until 37 B.C. His rule lasted over thirty years, ending with his death in 4 B.C.

Corrupt Character

For political advantage, Herod supported a legend fabricated by Nicolaus of Damascus, a friend who alleged Herod descended from a noble family whom King Nebuchadnezzar[268] had deported to Babylonia centuries earlier after conquering the Kingdom of Judah. (Josephus, 1977, p. 289)[269] The claim has no historical basis, for Herod had no Jewish ancestors, his father Antipater[270] an Edomite from Idumea and his mother Cypros an Arab

---

[266] Client king – ruler of a kingdom economically, politically, and militarily subordinate to another ruling power (A client kingdom of Rome possessed a lower political status than a Roman province.)

[267] A triumvirate consists of three persons serving as a ruling body.

[268] Nebuchadnezzar (nĕb-ü-khăd-nĕz-zər)

[269] *The Antiquities of the Jews*, Book 14, Chapter 2, Paragraph 3; Titus Flavius Josephus (jō-sĕ́-fəs), a Jewish general and historian, lived 37-100 A.D. For more information regarding Josephus, see "Appendix 3: Glossary."

[270] Antipater (ăn-tĭ́-pə-tər)

from Nabatea. Both Idumea and Nabatea lay south of the Kingdom of Judah conquered by Nebuchadnezzar.

Devious conspiracies, relentless feuds, murders, and incessant immorality characterized Herod's rule. Born into this fiery political environment, Jesus faced immediate danger due to Herod's paranoia. Herod executed many of his own close relatives whom he perceived as political threats and remained true to character when he ordered the murder of the boys of Bethlehem[271] in an attempt to kill "the One who has been born King of the Jews,"[272] the Child sought by the Magi.

The biblical scholar Merrill Unger aptly portrayed Herod's traits when he wrote,

> *Herod was not only an Idumaean in race and a Jew in religion, but he was a heathen in practice and a monster in character ... and on the merest suspicion put to death his favorite wife, Mariamne ... and also her sons, Aristobulus and Alexander ... and at last, when on his own deathbed, just five days before he died, he ordered his son Antipater to be slain.* (Unger, 1988, heading *Her'od the Great*, subheading *Character*)

Herod's Death

Herod the Great died at the age of 69 in the city of Jericho the spring of 4 B.C., between March 23 and April 11. His family buried him at Herodium, a palace-fortress located four miles[273] southeast of Bethlehem. The calculation of the time Herod died corrects for an error made by Dionysius Exiguus[274] and considers the dates of the eclipse and Passover discussed below.

In 525 A.D., Exiguus developed the *Anno Domini* (A.D.) dating system.[275] He computed the start of the Roman emperor Augustus' reign as four years later than it actually began. Consequently, his calculation that

---

[271] Matthew 2:16

[272] Matthew 2:2 BT

[273] Six kilometers

[274] Dionysius Exiguus (dī-ŭ-nĭ-shē-ŭs ĕg-zĭ-gyū-wŭs) – a Catholic monk who resided in Rome

[275] A.D. abbreviates *Anno Domini*, the Latin phrase meaning "year of our Lord." B.C. abbreviates *before Christ*, the meaning of the Latin phrase *Ante Christum*.

Herod the Great died in 1 A.D. erred by four years as well. Herod died in 4 B.C.

Flavius Josephus,[276] a first-century historian, recorded that a lunar eclipse occurred not long before Herod's death. (Josephus, 1977, p. 365)[277] That total lunar eclipse took place the night of March 23, 4 B.C., 7:30 p.m. to 9:12 p.m.[278]

Josephus also wrote that Herod's son, Archelaus,[279] crushed a revolt immediately prior to the Passover festivities following Herod's death. (Josephus, 1977, pp. 367-368)[280] That Passover celebration began on April 11, 4 B.C.

Accordingly, the date of Herod's death fell in the spring of 4 B.C., after the eclipse of March 23 but before the Passover of April 11.

Judea (Matthew 2:1)

Kingdom of Judea

Between the years 598 B.C. and 586 B.C., King Nebuchadnezzar of Babylonia invaded the Kingdom of Judah three times. During the final invasion in 586 B.C., he demolished Jerusalem. Throughout those years, the Babylonians deported large numbers of Judeans who reluctantly colonized various regions of the Babylonian Empire. Following the death of Nebuchadnezzar in 562 B.C., three more kings succeeded him before Babylonia fell to Persia.

King Cyrus of Persia conquered Babylonia in 539 B.C. and annexed the Babylonian Empire into his domain. Cyrus allowed the

---

[276] Titus Flavius Josephus, a Jewish general and historian, lived 37-100 A.D. For more information regarding Josephus, see "Appendix 3: Glossary."

[277] *The Antiquities of the Jews*, Book 17, Chapter 7, Paragraph 4

[278] The *Javascript Lunar Eclipse Explorer* tool on the NASA (National Aeronautics and Space Administration) web page http://eclipse.gsfc.nasa.gov/JLEX/JLEX-AS.html calculated the date and time of this lunar eclipse as seen from Jerusalem the spring of 4 B.C.

[279] Archelaus (är-khǝ-lắ-ŭs); For additional information regarding Archelaus, see "Chapter 7 – Going Home," headings "Archelaus Was Ruler (Matthew 2:22)" and "Afraid to Go There (Matthew 2:22)."

[280] *The Antiquities of the Jews*, Book 17, Chapter 9, Paragraphs 1-3

Judeans in Babylonian territories to return to their homeland, his policy concerning ethnic groups displaced by previous conquerors. In addition, he issued a decree committing his own government to fund the reconstruction of the Temple in Jerusalem. (Josephus, 1977, p. 228)[281]

Even so, most of the families Nebuchadnezzar had deported from the Kingdom of Judah chose to remain in the Babylonian territories to which they had relocated. The majority of those who returned to their native land belonged to the tribe of Judah. This led the Gentile[282] world to refer to the homeland of the Jews as *Judea*. The Greco-Roman[283] name *Judea* signified "land of Judah," one of the original tribes of Israel.[284]

In 332 B.C., Alexander the Great conquered Judea, incorporated it into his Macedonian Empire, and introduced Greek cultural influence to the region.[285] Following Alexander's death in 323 B.C., subsequent Hellenistic[286] kingdoms absorbed Judea. In 167 B.C., Judea revolted and three years later established itself as an independent kingdom ruled by the Hasmonean dynasty, a Jewish family of priestly heritage.

In 63 B.C., the Roman army occupied Judea, and Rome claimed it as a client[287] state. Over the next 20 years and more, Rome struggled to stabilize the turbulent political environment within Judea. In 39 B.C., the Roman Senate elected Herod the Great monarch of the Kingdom of Judea and sent him to secure the region. After leading a two-year military assault, Herod effectively began his reign as King of Judea in 37 B.C. Judea continued under Rome's imperial dominion at the time of Jesus' birth and

---

[281] *The Antiquities of the Jews*, Book 11, Chapter 1, Paragraph 2; Ezra 1:1-11

[282] The Jews identified anyone not of Jacob's bloodline as a Gentile. God gave Jacob, son of Isaac and grandson of Abraham, the name *Israel* (Genesis 32:28).

[283] The phrase "Greco-Roman" refers to something characteristic of both the ancient Greek and ancient Roman cultures.

[284] Genesis 49:1-33

[285] The extensive influence of Greek culture resulting from Alexander the Great's widespread conquests led the New Testament writers to compose their literature and correspondence in the Greek language.

[286] "Hellenistic" refers to anything relating to Greek influence dating after Alexander the Great's death in 323 B.C. (e.g., history, culture, art).

[287] Client state – a kingdom economically, politically, and militarily subordinate to another ruling power (A client kingdom of Rome possessed a lower political status than a Roman province.)

for hundreds of years thereafter.

Tetrarchy of Judea

Herod the Great revised his will shortly before dying the spring of 4 B.C., bequeathing the majority of his kingdom to his three surviving sons. Caesar Augustus, the final authority regarding the future of the Kingdom of Judea, honored Herod's desires and divided the kingdom into tetrarchies.[288] To Philip he gave the Roman regions of Batanea, Iturea, Trachonitis, Gaulanitis, and Auranitis (about one fourth of the territory inherited by Herod's sons), assigning him the title Tetrarch of Batanea.[289] Antipas received the title Tetrarch of Galilee, together with the regions of Galilee and Perea (about one fourth of the territory inherited by Herod's sons). Archelaus obtained the regions of Samaria, Judea, and Idumea (about two fourths of the territory inherited by Herod's sons), accepting the title Ethnarch[290] of the Tetrarchy of Judea.

---

[288] Tetrarchy – one fourth of a Roman client kingdom or province
[289] Tetrarch – "Ruler of a Fourth"
[290] Ethnarch – "Ruler of a Nation"

Map: Territory Inherited by Herod's Sons[291]

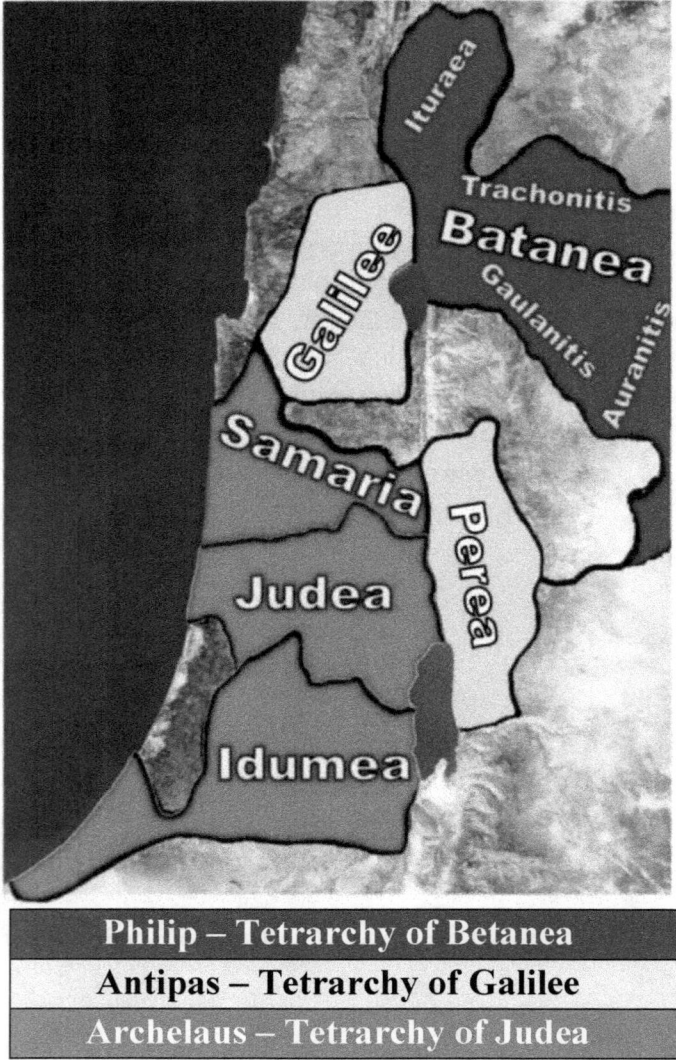

Philip – Tetrarchy of Betanea
Antipas – Tetrarchy of Galilee
Archelaus – Tetrarchy of Judea

Figure 4 - 1

---

[291] Sections of Herod's kingdom not assigned to Herod's three sons by Caesar Augustus do not relate to the story of Jesus. He gave a small portion to Herod's sister Salome, and merged the remainder into the Province of Syria.

Province of Judea

The corrupt, ineffective leadership of Archelaus eventually led Caesar Augustus to remove him from office and exile him to the city of Vienne, Gaul in 6 A.D. At the same time, Augustus replaced Archelaus with Coponius, a Roman prefect,[292] and created the Roman Province[293] of Judea from the territory Archelaus had governed. The province encompassed three regions – *Samaria,* the most northern region, *Judea,* located immediately to the south of Samaria, and *Idumea,* directly south of Judea. Separate from the Province of Judea, Antipas continued to govern the Tetrarchy of Galilee and Philip remained the Tetrarch of Batanea.

Map: Roman Province of Judea

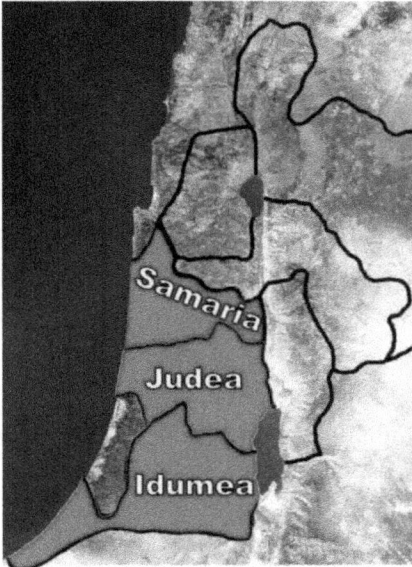

Figure 4 - 2

---

[292] Prefect – the title of high-ranking military or civil officials performing various functions within the Roman Empire [Coponius served as the first of seven Roman prefects governing the Province of Judea (Pontius Pilate the fifth). Agrippa I ruled as *King of all Judea* after the seventh prefect, followed by eight procurators (higher ranking officials than prefects). Finally, 14 legates governed Judea (military generals, higher ranking than procurators).]

[293] A province served as the basic administrative unit of the Roman Empire outside the peninsula of Italy.

What About Palestine?

The Nemesis

Ancient historians originally used the word *Palestine* (a.k.a., Philistia) to refer to the southern seacoast of the land of Canaan inhabited by the Philistines. Following the conquest of that region by Israel, the Philistines continued to control a smaller coastal region to the west of Jerusalem along the Mediterranean Sea. It extended from the city of Joppa southward to the city of Gaza, with the cities of Ashkelon, Ashdod, and Gath[294] lying in between.

The Israelites called the land of the Philistines *Palásheth* (päl-ă-shĕth),[295] meaning "break through," in the sense of invaders. Philistia, an evil nation, proved a nemesis of Israel throughout most of its history. Even so, God chose to leave a remnant of Philistia in place to use as a tool to discipline the people of Israel when He saw the need.[296]

The Great Revolt

In the early 70's A.D., the Romans suppressed a Judean revolt and another in 117 A.D. In 132 A.D., the Jews initiated the *Great Revolt*,[297] which the Roman Army crushed in 135 A.D. Subsequently, the Roman emperor Hadrian attempted to abolish any residue of Jewish nationalism. Toward that end, he consolidated the provinces of Syria and Judea, naming the new province *Syria Palestina* (i.e., land of Syria Palestine),[298] and designated the Syrian city of Antioch its capital. Hadrian's action delivered a tremendous emotional blow to the Jews, who found their homeland

---

[294] Gath – the hometown of the giant Goliath, pride of the Philistine army until God brought him down with a stone hurled from David's sling (1 Samuel 17:1-58)

[295] Palásheth (päl-ă-shĕth), פְּלֶשֶׁת; Biblical translators most often render this Hebrew word as Philistia, rarely as Palestine. For instance, the King James Version renders *Palásheth* once as Palestine, three times as Palestina, and three times as Philistia.

[296] Judges 2:20-3:3

[297] The Great Revolt, also called the Bar Kokhba Revolt

[298] In the 5th century B.C., Herodotus referred to the entire area bordering the eastern Mediterranean Sea northeast of Egypt and south of Phoenicia as Palestinian Syria and he called the Israelites living within that region Palestinian Syrians. However, during Jesus' lifetime on Earth, the name *Judea* applied to the southern expanse within that region.

named after their perennial enemy, the Philistines.

Hadrian also changed the name of Jerusalem to *Aelia Capitolina*,[299] dedicating the metropolis to the Roman god Jupiter and exiling all Jews from the city and its surrounding area.

Jerusalem (Matthew 2:1)

Melchizedek's Salem

Some 2,000 years before Herod's rule, during Abraham's[300] era, inhabitants of the Jerusalem site called their city "Salem."[301] Melchizedek, a priest of God, reigned as king of Salem. In recognition of Melchizedek's spiritual role, Abraham honored him with one tenth of the spoils of the battle through which Abraham rescued Lot (Abraham's nephew) from the King of Elam.[302]

Zion

The town's first inhabitants settled on Zion, the highest of five rocky hills over which Jerusalem spread as it developed. In Scripture, the word *Zion* varies in meaning, depending on the immediate context[303] in which a writer used the term. Scripture often employs *Zion* as a generic reference to the entire metropolis of Jerusalem.[304] Prophets sometimes referred to the whole nation of Israel as Zion.[305] In the New Testament, Zion refers figuratively to the church.[306]

---

[299] Hadrian devised *Aelia* from his surname, Aelius. Likewise, he derived *Capitolina* from the Capitoline Triad of Roman gods – Jupiter, Juno, and Minerva.

[300] Known as Abram at the time of his meeting with Melchizedek (Genesis 14:14-20), God later changed Abram's name to Abraham (Genesis 17:5).

[301] Psalm 76:1-2

[302] Genesis 14:14-20; Hebrews 7:4

[303] Context, the communication before and after a word or passage, often sheds light on the meaning intended by the writer or speaker.

[304] 1 Kings, 8:1; 1 Chronicles 11:5; Isaiah 30:19; Psalm 48:2,11-12

[305] Isaiah 59:20; Zechariah 9:13

[306] Hebrews 12:22-24

Religious & Political Importance

Jerusalem, the primary city of the Judean region, numbered around 50,000 inhabitants during Jesus' time on Earth. Located 33 miles[307] east of the Mediterranean Sea and 15 miles[308] west of the Dead Sea, Jerusalem had no seaport. In spite of its inland terrain and rocky, infertile countryside, Jerusalem became a prominent city stimulated by religion and politics, inseparable within the Jewish culture of the first century. God's Temple, the central attraction in Jerusalem, brought supreme importance to the city, and religious issues greatly affected the political environment. As a result, Herod the Great established his primary residence in Jerusalem, hub of the Jewish culture, instead of the Mediterranean coastal city of Caesarea, which served as the Roman center of activities.

Map: Jerusalem

Figure 4 - 3

---

[307] 53 kilometers
[308] 24 kilometers

Dome of the Rock – Muslim Mosque on Jewish Temple Mount (1936 A.D.)

Figure 4 - 4

Jerusalem (Looking West About 1931 A.D.)

Figure 4 - 5

Jerusalem (About 1935 A.D.)

Figure 4 - 6

Jerusalem (About 1890 A.D.)

Figure 4 - 7

Jerusalem (About 1919 A.D.)

Figure 4 - 8

Jerusalem Vegetable Market (About 1900 A.D.)

Figure 4 - 9

Bethlehem (Matthew 2:1)

Historical Significance

Like Jerusalem, Bethlehem lay within the region of Judea. For so small a town, it possessed great historical significance. The inspiring story of Ruth occurred in that village.[309] Bethlehem gained subsequent fame as the hometown of King David, the giant killer.[310] Above all, the birth of the Messiah took place there.[311]

Map: Bethlehem

Figure 4 - 10

---

[309] Ruth 1:1-2,19,22; 2:4; 4:11
[310] I Samuel 17:12
[311] Matthew 2:1

Bethlehem (1931 A.D.)

Figure 4 - 11

Bethlehem (About 1890 A.D.)

Figure 4 - 12

Bethlehem (About 1898 A.D.)

Figure 4 - 13

Bethlehem (About 1919 A.D.)

Figure 4 - 14

Census

Prior to Jesus' birth, Caesar Augustus ordered Roman officials to take a census of the Roman Empire.[312] Personal data collected during the census served as part of an accounting system ensuring proper taxation of all subjects. Rome collected an annual poll tax[313] of one denarius[314] from males aged 14-65 and females aged 12-65, in addition to other levies and tolls. (Edersheim, 1881, pp. 53-54) Consequently, Rome required both men and women to register in the census. Roman citizens did not have to pay the poll tax.

Front of an "Emperor Tiberius" Denarius (Minted 20 A.D.)

Figure 4 - 15 (C. Bagby Collection)

---

[312] Luke 2:1-5

[313] Poll tax – a fixed amount each individual must pay; poll means "head" (i.e., head tax)

[314] Denarius – a small silver Roman coin about ¾-inch (2 centimeters) in diameter, worth one day's manual labor in Judea

Back of an "Emperor Tiberius" Denarius (Minted 20 A.D.)

Figure 4 - 16 (C. Bagby Collection)

Jews maintained genealogical records within the civil registry of their family's ancestral hometown. Therefore, registering for the census required each individual to travel to the municipality of their principal ancestor. Joseph and Mary, both "of the house and family of David,"[315] had a common grandfather who descended from David.[316] Accordingly, Luke states Joseph journeyed to Bethlehem "in order to register *along with Mary*"[317] to complete their legal obligation.

Luke disclosed that Joseph and Mary remained engaged[318] when

---

[315] Luke 2:4 NASU; Matthew 1:6,16; Luke 3:23,31

[316] For more information about the related bloodlines of Joseph and Mary, see "Chapter 2 – Kings & Scoundrels: Jesus' Ancestors," heading "Jacob Fathered Joseph (Matthew 1:16)," subheading "Overlapping Family Lines."

[317] Luke 2:5 NASU

[318] For a discussion of marriage engagement customs among Jews of the first century A.D., see "Chapter 3 – Birth of Jesus, Rescuer of His People," heading "Engaged (Matthew 1:18)."

they left Nazareth,[319] not yet married. Nevertheless, Joseph cared for Mary and the unborn Child as a loving husband and father should, while they traveled to Bethlehem.[320] Thus God used the Roman census to ensure Mary delivered her baby in Bethlehem instead of Nazareth, fulfilling Micah 5:2-5, a prophecy that foretold the Messiah would be born in Bethlehem.

***

Contemplation Points

1. Given Mary's physical condition, why do you think she decided to make the trip to Bethlehem instead of remaining in Nazareth?
2. Do you fulfill inconvenient legal obligations as Mary did?
   a. If so, explain why.
   b. If not, explain why not.

Magi from the East (Matthew 2:1)

Who Were the Magi?

Upon Jesus' birth,[321] the Magi began their journey from a region far northeast of Judea. The Scriptures tell us nothing more about their land of origin. However, the writings of other ancient historians reveal the Magi's identity and their homeland.

Herodotus,[322] a Greek historian who lived in the fifth century B.C., mentioned the Magi. Modern scholars commonly refer to Herodotus as the "father of history." He wrote,

> *Deioces collected the Medes[323] into one nation, and ruled over that. The following are the tribes of the Medes: the Busae, Parataceni, Struchates,*

---

[319] Luke 2:5

[320] For information about the legal status of a couple engaged according to Jewish custom, see "Chapter 3 – Birth of Jesus, Rescuer of His People," heading "Engaged (Matthew 1:18)."

[321] For a discussion of when the Magi arrived in Bethlehem, see "Chapter 4 – The Magi Meet Herod, King of Judea," heading "His Star (Matthew 2:2)," subheading "When did the Magi Arrive in Bethlehem?"

[322] Herodotus (hě-rŏ-dŏ-tŭs)

[323] Medes lived in the nation of Media, the political center of the Median Empire.

Arizanti, Budii, and the Magi. (Herodotus, 1848, p. 46)[324]

Median Empire and the Magi

The *Magh*[325] tribe lived in the Madai (Media) region of the Median Empire, about 800 air miles[326] northeast of Bethlehem, a caravan journey of at least 1,300 miles.[327] Historians refer to a member of the Magh tribe as a Magus and to more than one member by the plural *Magi*.

Magi served the Median king as priests and counselors. Their intellectual pursuits encompassed philosophy, medicine, natural science, and astronomy. They centered their activities in Ecbatana, the capital city of the Median Empire. Pliny the Elder, a first-century Roman historian, referred to the Magh home as "the town Ecbatana belonging to the Magi." (Pliny, 1848, p. 139)

Map: Median Empire & Madai Region – Homeland of the Magi

Figure 4 - 17

---

[324] *The Histories of Herodotus*, Book 1, Paragraph 101
[325] Magh (mäg) – Persian word meaning "powerful"
[326] 1,300 kilometers
[327] 2,100 kilometers

Persian Empire and the Magi

Astyages[328] ruled the Median Empire 584-550 B.C. In 558 B.C., he appointed his grandson Cyrus to succeed Cambyses[329] as ruler of the Persian district of Anshan. Five years later, Cyrus initiated a rebellion against his grandfather (553 B.C.).

After three years of revolt, the Persians captured King Astyages in 550 B.C., and Cyrus seized control of the Median Empire. He aggressively established a *Persian Empire*, sometimes referred to as the Medo-Persian Empire.[330] Historians refer to him as *Cyrus the Great*.

Having won the loyalty of the Median Magi, Cyrus appointed them to serve Persian royalty as priests, counselors, and tutors.

Intent on building the world's preeminent kingdom, Cyrus expanded his Persian Empire, pushing southward to conquer the Babylonian Empire. His new Babylonian territory encompassed the land of Judea, within which lay Bethlehem, the future birthplace of the Messiah.

Map: Persian Empire

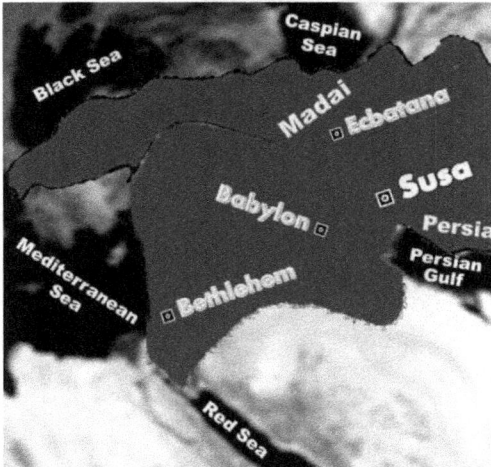

Figure 4 - 18

Subsequent Empires and the Magi

The Persian Empire fell to Alexander the Great and became part of his Macedonian Empire (336 B.C. – 323 B.C.). Upon Alexander's death, his generals conspired against one another for control, fracturing his empire. Seleucus I Nicator,[331] one of those generals, took possession of the eastern region of Alexander's empire, ruling what developed into the Seleucid[332] Empire (312 B.C. – 63 B.C.), within which lay the Magi homeland.

Map: Seleucid Empire

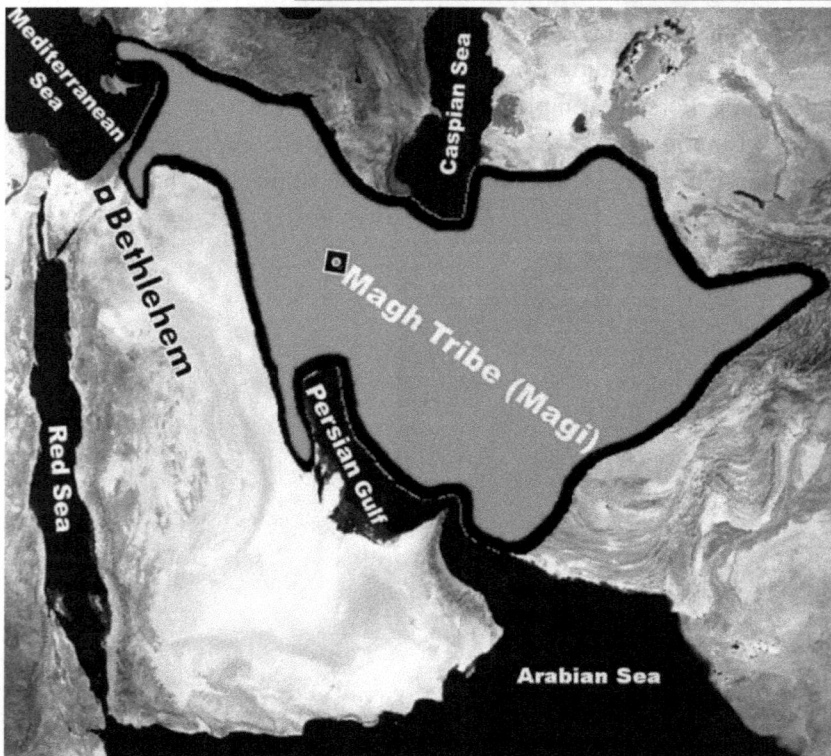

Figure 4 - 19

---

[331] Seleucus I Nicator (sě-lü-kŭs nĭ́-kā-tər)
[332] Seleucid (sě-lü-sĭd)

Several decades later, as the Seleucid Empire began to weaken, its Parthia province broke away, declaring independence.

Map: Parthia Province of Seleucid Empire

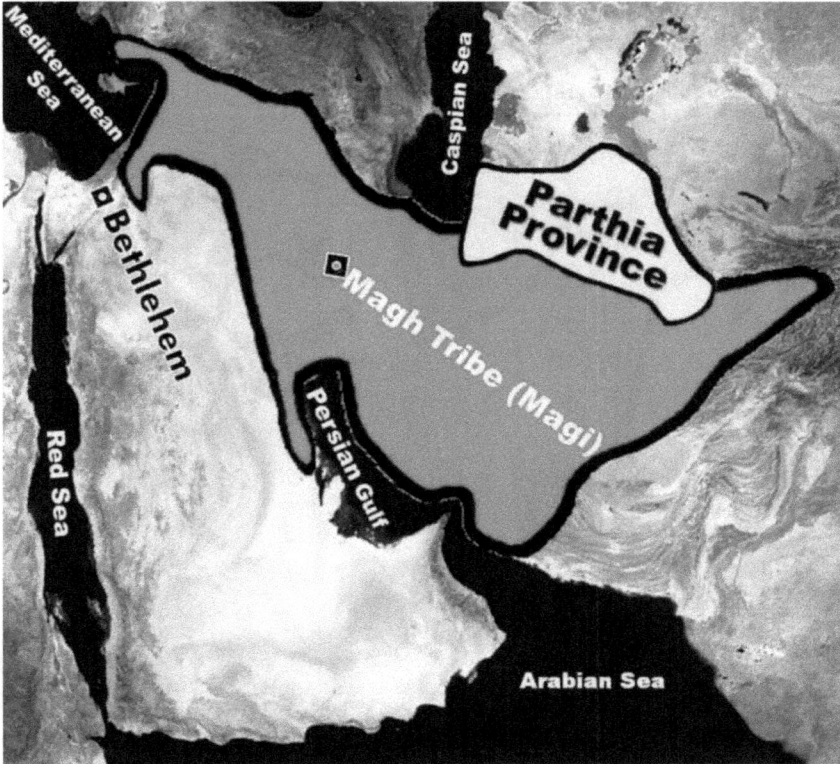

Figure 4 - 20

However, Parthia lacked the military strength to defend itself against invaders. In 238 B.C., the nomadic Parni[333] tribe led by Arsaces I[334] invaded Parthia from the northeast and conquered it. Arsaces assimilated Parni culture into Parthia's culture and maintained Parthian identity for his new realm.

Map: Parni Conquest of Parthia

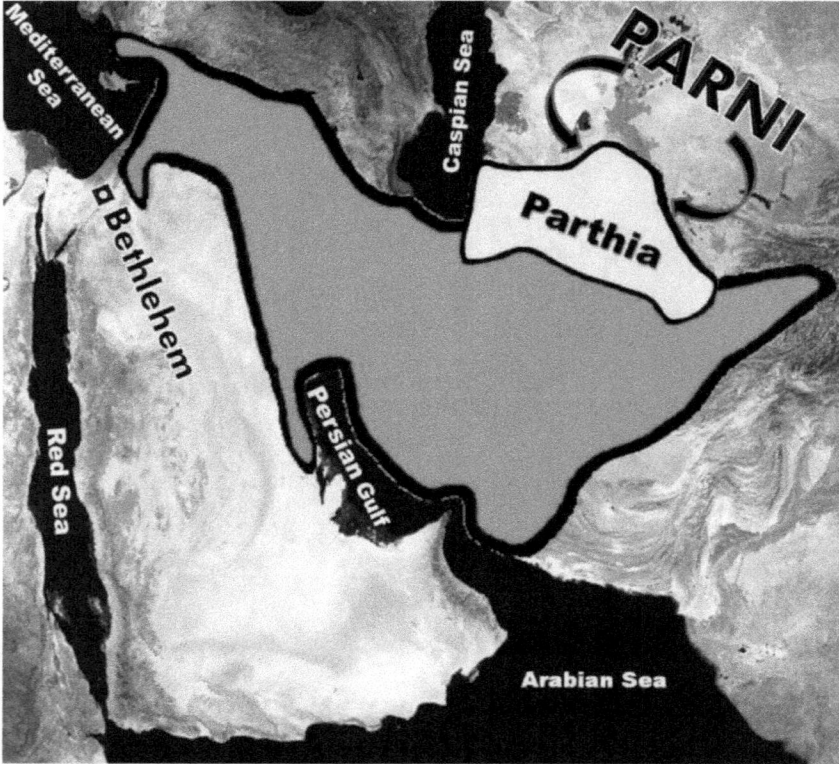

Figure 4 - 21

---

[333] Parni (pár-nī)
[334] Arsaces I (ár-sə-sēz)

As Parthia expanded its territory southward and westward through conquests, the Magi found their homeland engulfed by the Parthian Empire (247 B.C. – 224 A.D.).

Map: Parthian Empire (1 A.D.)

Figure 4 - 22

By the time of Jesus' birth, the Parthian Empire and the Roman Empire had positioned themselves as superpower rivals. Parthia had conquered the Asian lands in the East extending from Syria to India, and Rome ruled the Western regions surrounding the Mediterranean Sea.

Map: Roman Empire & Parthian Empire (1 A.D.)

Figure 4 - 23

Parthian Empire and the Magi

By the time Magi visited the child Jesus around 6-4 B.C.,[335] their tribe had belonged to the Parthian Empire for over two centuries. No longer merely counselors to royalty, the Magi had attained powerful political influence. As noted by the Greek historian Strabo, who lived from about 64 B.C. to 24 A.D.,

> *The council of the Parthians is composed of two classes, one of relatives, (of the royal family,) and another of ... magi, by both of which kings are chosen.*[336] (Strabo, 1856, p. 251)

Hence, Magi would have served as part of the national council that elected King Phraates IV,[337] who reigned over the Parthian Empire from 37 – 2 B.C., overlapping the date of Jesus' birth.[338]

Magi's Source of Knowledge

The Magi identified the unfamiliar star in the eastern sky as a sign the birth of the King of the Jews had taken place.[339] They understood Him to be divine and worthy of their worship. Yet, how did they become so well informed?

The Magi could have gained partial knowledge about the coming King of the Jews from the writings of God's prophets. Given their diverse intellectual pursuits, they may have possessed copies of the Jewish Scriptures.[340] Even so, no Messianic prophecy within the Scriptures

---

[335] For a discussion of when the Magi arrived in Bethlehem, see "Chapter 5 – The Magi Meet Jesus, King of the Jews," heading "The Star Stood Above Where the Child Was (Matthew 2:9)," subheading "Date of Jesus' Birth" and subheading "When Did the Magi Arrive in Bethlehem?"

[336] *Geographica* by Strabo, Book XI, Chapter IX, Section 3

[337] Phraates (frä-ă-tās)

[338] For a discussion of the date of Jesus' birth, see "Chapter 5 – The Magi Meet Jesus, King of the Jews," heading "The Star Stood Above Where the Child Was (Matthew 2:9)," subheading "Date of Jesus' Birth."

[339] Matthew 2:2

[340] Various Gentile seekers of God outside the borders of Judea possessed copies of the Scriptures. For example, the Treasurer of Ethiopia sat in his chariot reading a scroll of Isaiah as his driver steered homeward from Jerusalem (Acts 8:26-38).

mentions a related star.

Their understanding of the star could have come through divine revelation. Upon completing their visit to Bethlehem, the Magi were "warned in a dream not to return to Herod."[341] Since that warning came from God, perhaps He had explained the star to them as well.

By whatever means the Magi learned of the birth of the King of the Jews, they clearly lived as spiritual men, because they

- Journeyed to a distant land to worship the divine Child,[342]
- Paid homage to Jesus, giving Him treasures,[343] and
- Obeyed God's warning not to return to Herod.[344]

What made the Magi so spiritually aware? What touched their hearts to make them so spiritually receptive? The prophet Daniel likely had a godly influence on the ancestors of those Magi – an influence still effectual at the time of Jesus' birth, some 550 years later. The series of events that led to Daniel's contact with the Magi of Media began in Babylon.

---

[341] Matthew 2:12 BT
[342] Matthew 2:1-2
[343] Matthew 2:11
[344] Matthew 2:12

The Daniel Connection

Daniel's Rise in the Babylonian Empire

Daniel arrived in Babylon as a captive,[345] deported from the Kingdom of Judah along with thousands of other Judahites following King Nebuchadnezzar's[346] conquest. A team of wise men served Nebuchadnezzar as he ruled the Babylonian Empire (605-562 B.C.). Impressed with Daniel's character and ability, Nebuchadnezzar appointed him leader of the wise men.[347]

Regardless, Nebuchadnezzar failed to prepare the way for a strong successor. For years following his death in 562 B.C., men of power and influence struggled for dominance over Babylonia. Initially, Nebuchadnezzar's young son Evil-Merodach succeeded him. The boy reigned for a little over two years (562-560 B.C.) before his brother-in-law, Neriglissar, killed him.

After his murder of Evil-Merodach, Neriglissar ruled from 560-556 B.C. Upon his death by natural cause, his young son Labashi-Marduk succeeded him. The boy reigned nine months until assassinated through a conspiracy instigated by Nabonidus.

Nabonidus, one of Nebuchadnezzar's sons-in-law, usurped the throne and reigned from 556-539 B.C. However, he preferred not to reside in Babylon, the capital city. Instead, he delegated control of Babylon to his son Belshazzar and appointed him co-ruler of the empire.

During a royal party the night of October 12, 539 B.C., a mysterious hand appeared by itself and wrote a four-word message on the plaster of the banquet hall. Belshazzar, with his knees literally shaking from fear, summoned Daniel to decipher the writing. Daniel explained that the message foretold the fall of the Babylonian Empire to the Persians.[348]

---

[345] For more information about the deportation of Judahites to Babylonia, see "Chapter 2 – Kings & Scoundrels: Jesus' Ancestors," heading "The Babylonian Deportation (Matthew 1:11)."

[346] Nebuchadnezzar (nĕb-ü-khăd-nĕz-zər)

[347] Daniel 2:48; Take care not to confuse the *wise men* of Nebuchadnezzar, king of the Babylonian Empire, with the *Magi* of Cyrus, king of the Persian Empire.

[348] Daniel 5:1-28

Belshazzar, second only to his father in power, immediately made Daniel the third most powerful leader of Babylonia. As the Scriptures explain,

> *Belshazzar gave orders, and they clothed Daniel with purple ... and issued a proclamation concerning him that he now had authority as the third ruler in the kingdom.*[349]

That very night, the army of Cyrus the Great, king of the Persian Empire, launched a surprise attack on Babylon.[350] Josephus[351] recorded that Belshazzar was "taken" at the time the Persian army conquered Babylon and that this resulted in "the end of the posterity of King Nebuchadnezzar." (Josephus, 1977, p. 226)[352] Thus, the army of Cyrus the Great took the life of Belshazzar the same night he had seen the handwriting appear on his wall.[353]

---

[349] Daniel 5:29 NASU

[350] October 12, 539 B.C.

[351] Titus Flavius Josephus (jō-sḗ-fəs), a Jewish general and historian, lived 37-100 A.D. For more information regarding Josephus, see "Appendix 3: Glossary."

[352] *The Antiquities of the Jews*, Book 10, Chapter 21, Paragraph 4

[353] Daniel 5:30

Daniel's Rise in the Persian Empire

Seventeen days later, Cyrus the Great entered victoriously into the city of Babylon.[354] Persian cuneiform[355] inscriptions confirm that Cyrus succeeded Belshazzar as ruler over Babylon. Shortly thereafter, Cyrus delegated the rule of Babylonia to Gubaru.[356]

Before Cyrus appointed him ruler of Babylonia, Gubaru had served as governor of Gutium, a region within the land of Media, just north of the fallen Babylonian Empire. Josephus called Gubaru by the name Darius[357] and mentioned he had family ties with Cyrus the Great. (Josephus, 1977, p. 226)[358]

Josephus also wrote that Darius (Gubaru) was 62 years old when made ruler of Babylon. (Josephus, 1977, p. 226)[359] Daniel, likewise, in his book within the Scriptures, reported Darius to be 62 when "made king."[360] Darius governed Babylonia on behalf of Cyrus the Great from 539-525 B.C.

According to Josephus, Darius selected three "presidents" to govern his 360 provinces. (Josephus, 1977, p. 226)[361] Daniel referred to these presidents as "commissioners."[362] Darius chose Daniel as one of the three commissioners who presided over the realm of Babylonia.[363]

---

[354] October 29, 539 B.C.

[355] Cuneiform, a system of writing developed by the ancient Sumerian culture of southern Mesopotamia, emerged about 3100 B.C. For more information concerning cuneiform, see "Appendix 3: Glossary."

[356] Historians also refer to Gubaru by the names Ugbaru and Gobryas, as well as Darius.

[357] Daniel refers to Gubaru by the name Darius six times (Daniel 6:1,6,9,25,28; 9:1) and twice as "Darius the Mede" (Daniel 5:31; 11:1).

[358] *The Antiquities of the Jews*, Book 10, Chapter 21, Paragraph 4

[359] *The Antiquities of the Jews*, Book 10, Chapter 21, Paragraph 4

[360] Daniel 5:31 NASU

[361] *The Antiquities of the Jews*, Book 10, Chapter 21, Paragraph 4

[362] Daniel 6:1-3 NASU

[363] Daniel 6:1-3

Eventually, Darius gave Daniel responsibility for all Babylonia.[364] Josephus commented that Darius held "Daniel in very great esteem, and made him the principal of his friends." (Josephus, 1977, p. 227)[365]

Josephus wrote further that Darius "took Daniel the prophet, and carried him with him into Media, and honoured him very greatly, and kept him with him." (Josephus, 1977, p. 226)[366] Three paragraphs later Josephus noted,

> *When Daniel was become so illustrious and famous, on account of the opinion of men had that he was beloved of God, he built a tower at Ecbatana, in Media: it was a most elegant building, and wonderfully made, and it is still remaining, and preserved to this day ... Now they bury the kings of Media, of Persia, and Parthia, in this tower, to this day; and he who was intrusted with the care of it, was a Jewish priest; which thing is also observed to this day.* (Josephus, 1977, p. 227)[367]

Darius (Gubaru) ensured Daniel held a high-ranking position in Media (Madai), specifically in its principal city Ecbatana, home of the Magi. During the course of his duties, Daniel would have met with the Magi on the occasions Persian rulers sought their counsel. Undoubtedly, he had a godly influence over those trusted advisors.

Some 550 years later, descendants of the Magi of Daniel's era observed a peculiar star with a divine purpose.

---

[364] Daniel 6:3,28
[365] *The Antiquities of the Jews*, Book 10, Chapter 21, Paragraph 7
[366] *The Antiquities of the Jews*, Book 10, Chapter 21, Paragraph 4
[367] *The Antiquities of the Jews*, Book 10, Chapter 21, Paragraph 7

His Star (Matthew 2:2)

Magi Arrive in Jerusalem

As Parthian dignitaries,[368] the Magi delegation to Judea would have warranted a sizeable escort of soldiers to protect them and their costly cargo.[369] For about two months their caravan trekked across at least 1,300 miles[370] of rugged, foreign terrain as they followed the star. Upon their arrival in Jerusalem, the star vanished.

"Where is the One who has been born King of the Jews?"[371] they asked, expecting everyone to know of the child King. "We saw His star in the east and we came to worship Him."[372]

The uneasy dodging of the question would have puzzled the Magi. The people in the streets knew King Herod would react adversely to the Magi's presence and inquiry. Not only would he have felt threatened by the suggested existence of a rival king, but he would have had reservations regarding the small Parthian army camped outside the Jerusalem gates.

Skeptics' Opinions About the Star

Matthew remains the only historian who mentioned the star and the role it played guiding the journey of the Magi. Skeptics discount the appearance of the star as a natural phenomenon. Yet, the appearance of something *unnatural* caught the attention of the Magi, seasoned astronomers familiar with the normal events in nighttime skies.

Some suggest the orbits of Saturn and Jupiter had aligned, creating the impression of an extraordinarily bright star. However, ancient astronomers repeatedly observed the conjunction of those two planets.

---

[368] For a discussion of the political rank of the Magi, see "Chapter 4 – The Magi Meet Herod, King of Judea," heading "Magi from the East (Matthew 2:1)," subheading "Parthian Empire and the Magi."

[369] For a discussion of the treasures the Magi would present to Jesus, see "Chapter 5 – The Magi Meet Jesus, King of Jews," heading "They Offered Him Gifts (Matthew 2:11)."

[370] 2,100 kilometers

[371] Matthew 2:2 BT

[372] Matthew 2:2 BT

Johannes Kepler, recognized as the father of modern astronomy, calculated that Jupiter and Saturn converged three times in 7 B.C. alone.[373] Still, the two planets never draw close enough together to appear as a single bright star. The minimum distance between Jupiter and Saturn during any conjunction as viewed from Earth measures about one degree, approximately twice the Moon's diameter.

Jupiter & Saturn Conjunction[374]

Figure 4 - 24

Other skeptics propose a comet wandered near to Earth, slowly making its way across the sky. Ancient astronomers recognized comets, although sighting comets less often than the convergence of planets. Halley's Comet appeared in 12 B.C.

---

[373] *De Stella Nova in Pede Serpentarii*, by Joannis Keppleri (1606 A.D.)
[374] Jupiter-Saturn image courtesy of NASA

Hale-Bopp Comet[375]

Figure 4 - 25

Still others attribute the star to the appearance of a supernova, an exploding star glowing from far distant outer space. Ancient astronomers rarely observed supernovas. Chinese astronomers provided the first historical record of a supernova in 185 A.D.

Chinese astronomers also recorded the appearance of the most well known supernova, the Crab Nebula, in 1054 A.D. At that time, the light from the explosion shined so brightly that observers viewed it with the naked eye during daytime hours for over three weeks. Nevertheless, they did not *follow* it anywhere. Located light-years away, a supernova could not have led the Magi to the house within which the Child resided in Bethlehem. However, the star the Magi followed did just that.[376]

---

[375] Hale-Bopp comet image courtesy of Rainwater Observatory, 1 Fine Pl., French Camp, MS 39745

[376] Matthew 2:9-11

Supernova 1994D in the Outskirts of Galaxy NGC 4526[377]

Figure 4 - 26

The Magi developed expertise in many academic disciplines, including astronomy. Familiar with normal celestial occurrences, they would have noted that the unnatural star they tracked had no similarity to natural phenomena. The star they followed behaved uniquely.

Appearing first in the eastern sky, the star changed position, taking the Magi westward from their home in the Parthian Empire. After several weeks, they arrived in Jerusalem. Upon their departure from Jerusalem, the

---

[377] Supernova 1994D image courtesy of NASA/ESA Hubble Space Telescope

star steered the Magi southward five miles,[378] leading them to Bethlehem. In the end, it identified the very house God intended them to enter.[379] No alignment of planets, comet, or supernova can maneuver as the Magi's star did.

What Was the Star?

Inspired by the Holy Spirit,[380] Matthew chose the word "star" to describe the celestial anomaly tracked by the Magi and offered no explanation concerning its physical nature. Had the composition and features of the star related to God's message, He would have presented an explanation. Instead, God clarified His *purpose* for the star. It served as a navigational tool to guide the Magi to "the One who has been born King of the Jews."[381]

***

Contemplation Points

1. How is it that the Magi saw the star in the east, but traveled westward from their homeland?
2. Why did the Magi stop in Jerusalem? Could they not have continued to follow the star to Bethlehem?
3. How long might the Magi have remained in Jerusalem before traveling to Bethlehem?

Bethlehem of Judah (Matthew 2:5-6)

Upon hearing of the Magi's search for "the One who has been born King of the Jews,"[382] Herod desperately wanted to find the Child. He convened a meeting of the Jewish chief priests and scribes who referred him to a Scripture written by Micah the prophet. They advised him the Messiah's birth would take place,

---

[378] Eight kilometers
[379] Matthew 2:9-11
[380] 2 Timothy 3:16
[381] Matthew 2:2 BT
[382] Matthew 2:2 BT

*In Bethlehem of Judah, for it has been written through the prophet,
"And you Bethlehem of the land of Judah, you are not at all least
among the leaders of Judah. For, from you will come forth a
Leader who will shepherd My people, Israel."*[383]

The chief priests and scribes informed Herod the Messiah's birth would take place in Bethlehem of *Judah*, as distinguished from Bethlehem of *Zebulun*. When God distributed the land of Canaan among the Israelites about 1,300 years earlier, He assigned the tribe of Judah a southern tract of land near the Dead Sea, while giving the tribe of Zebulun a northern territory near the Sea of Galilee.[384] A town named Bethlehem existed in both regions.

Who Were the Chief Priests? (Matthew 2:4)

Herod summoned the chief priests for advice, but who were the chief priests? Insufficient historical documentation exists to determine how the organization of chief priests developed or the date it began. Old Testament books lack any reference to the group. Mark became the first biblical writer to mention the chief priests when he wrote his biography of Jesus in the 50s A.D.[385]

Through King David, God divided the priesthood into 24 divisions under His Covenant with the nation of Israel.[386] Discontent with God's organizational design for the priesthood, Jewish religious leaders modified it by creating the society of *chief priests*. The association included the current high priest, his deputy, any living man who had held the position of high priest, and the leader of each of the 24 divisions of priests. The chief priests also counted themselves among the members of the Council,[387] another man-made religious institution sometimes called the Sanhedrin or Sanhedrim.[388]

---

[383] Matthew 2:5-6 BT; Micah 5:2-5
[384] Joshua 19:15-16
[385] Mark 8:31
[386] 1 Chronicles 24:1-31; Luke mentioned that the priest Zacharias, Elizabeth's husband and the father of John the Immerser, belonged to the division of Abijah (Luke 1:5).
[387] Luke 22:66
[388] For additional information about the Council, see "Appendix 3: Glossary."

Who Were the Scribes? (Matthew 2:4)

Herod called upon the scribes, in addition to the chief priests, to inquire where the Messiah's birth had occurred. The responsibilities of scribes evolved over ages. During Herod's era, their role varied greatly from the past.

Prior to the Babylonian deportation,[389] a scribe served as an officer in the king's court who documented legal statutes. In addition, he made copies of official manuscripts, distributing them as required. Familiar with the intent of the King's decrees, a scribe also served as a legal authority to clarify details of law for the public.

A different type of scribe emerged around 458 B.C., upon the return of the first Judahites to Judea from the Babylonian deportation. At that time, a priest named Ezra "set his heart to study the law of the Lord and to practice it, and to teach His statutes and ordinances."[390] He became "a scribe skilled in the Law of Moses, which the Lord God of Israel had given."[391]

Following Ezra's lead, others joined him in scribal endeavors. They meticulously produced copies of the Scriptures and taught the Word of God to their countrymen. Those godly scribes chose not to document their personal teachings,[392] fearing others might come to consider their remarks equal in authority to God's Scriptures. Hence, one generation passed down their lessons orally to the next generation. Simon the Just, the last of that company of scribes, died around 290 B.C., close to 180 years after Ezra began his work.

---

[389] For more information about the deportation of Israelites to Babylonia, see "Chapter 2 – Kings & Scoundrels: Jesus' Ancestors," heading "The Babylonian Deportation (Matthew 1:11)."

[390] Ezra 7:10 NASU

[391] Ezra 7:6 NASU

[392] Ezra, the only known priest of God among the scribes of his era (Nehemiah 8:2,9;12:26), also served as one of God's prophets and wrote the biblical book (Ezra) to convey a message God delivered through him, not to communicate his personal remarks (2 Peter 1:20-21).

In 140 B.C., about 150 years after the death of Simon the Just, a new breed of scribes surfaced. Joses ben Joezer[393] and Joses ben Jochanan[394] served as their first leaders. Although they began with righteous motives, they deemed it necessary to document the verbal instruction of the scribes who came before them, desiring to preserve the *traditional* teachings for posterity.

Regrettably, over the decades that followed, that new community of scribes compelled everyone to adhere to the traditional teachings of the ancient scribes. Some scribes aligned with the chief priests[395] who led the Sadducee sect,[396] while others allied with the Pharisees.[397] The Pharisaic scribes came to teach that the "traditions of the elders" *superseded* the authority of the Scriptures.[398]

Thus the perversion the scribes of Ezra's generation desired to avoid, that others might misrepresent their remarks as having equal authority to God's Scriptures, became an inexcusable reality. Jesus strongly condemned the practice of the scribes[399] of Herod's day.[400]

---

[393] Joses ben Joezer (jŏ-sĕ́s bĕn jŏ-ĕ́z-ər)

[394] Joses ben Jochanan (jŏ-sĕ́s bĕn jŏ-khô-nŏ́n)

[395] Matthew 2:4; Luke 22:2,66; Matthew 16:21; 20:18; 21:15; 26:57; 27:41; Mark 11:18,27; 14:1,43,53; 15:1,31; Luke 9:22; 19:47; 20:1,19; 23:10; Acts 4:5-6

[396] For more information concerning the Sadducee sect, see "Chapter 9 – Poisonous Snakes: Pharisees & Sadducees," heading "Who Were the Sadducees? (Matthew 3:7)."

[397] Mark 2:16; Luke 5:30; Acts 23:9; Matthew 5:20; 12:38; 15:1; 23:2,13-15,23,25,27,29; Mark 7:5; 8:31; Luke 5:21; 6:7; 11:53; 15:2; John 8:3; For more information concerning the Pharisee sect, see "Chapter 9 – Poisonous Snakes: Pharisees & Sadducees," heading "Who Were the Pharisees? (Matthew 3:7)."

[398] Matthew 15:2-3,6

[399] Scribes – also referred to as *lawyers*, in relation to the Law of Moses and the traditions of the elders (Matthew 22:35; Luke 7:30; 10:25; 11:45-46,52; 14:3)

[400] Mark 12:38-40; Luke 20:46-47

Review of Matthew's Text (Matthew 2:1-8)

₁ In the days of King Herod, after Jesus was born in Bethlehem of Judea, listen now, Magi from the East arrived in Jerusalem, ₂ saying, "Where is the One who has been born King of the Jews? We saw His star in the east and we came to worship Him."

₃ Having heard this, King Herod was troubled and all Jerusalem with him. ₄ Then, bringing together all the chief priests and scribes of the people, he was asking them where the Christ was to be born. ₅ They said to him, "In Bethlehem of Judah, for it has been written through the prophet, ₆ 'And you Bethlehem of the land of Judah, you are not at all least among the leaders of Judah; for from you will come forth a Leader who will shepherd My people, Israel.'"

₇ Then Herod, having called the Magi privately, learned from them the precise time of the appearance of the star. ₈ Later, sending them to Bethlehem, he said, "When you[401] get there, make detailed inquiries about the Child. Tell me when you find Him, so that I might also come to worship Him." (BT)

---

[401] To convey the intent of Matthew's Greek text, the BT marks *you* and *your* with a double underscore when plural (i.e., you, your).

....

CHAPTER 5

The Magi Meet Jesus, King of the Jews

The Magi answered King Herod's summons, probably expecting him to know where to find the Child, while Herod had already established the birth town, fearing the Child might be the Messiah long awaited by the Jews. Feigning a desire to worship "the One who has been born King of the Jews,"[402] Herod sent the Magi to Bethlehem with instructions to advise him of the Child's location.

Matthew's Text (Matthew 2:9-12)[403]

9 Having heeded the king, they traveled on their way. And look, the star that they saw in the east led the way before them until it stood above where the Child was. 10 They rejoiced with exceedingly great joy when they saw the star. 11 Upon entering the house, they saw the Child with Mary, His mother. After they fell down and worshipped Him, they opened their treasures and offered Him gifts of gold and frankincense and myrrh. 12 Then, having been warned in a dream not to return to Herod, they departed by another way to their own country. (BT)

---

[402] Matthew 2:2,8 BT
[403] No passages within the books of Mark, Luke, or John parallel Matthew 2:9-12.

Star Stood Above Where Child Was (Matthew 2:9)

Redirected from Jerusalem to Bethlehem by King Herod, the Magi "rejoiced with exceedingly great joy when they saw the star" reappear, leading them southward toward their destination.[404] Upon their arrival, the star altered its course a final time and "stood above where the Child was."[405] Yet, where did the Magi find Jesus?

The Caravan

God required all Israelite men to attend three annual religious festivals in Jerusalem, the Feast of Unleavened Bread (Passover), the Feast of Weeks (Pentecost), and the Feast of Booths (Tabernacles).[406] Dr. John Kitto points out, "Among the ancient Jews, the inhabitants of the same village or district would naturally form themselves into travelling parties, for mutual security as well as for enjoying the society of acquaintance." (Kitto, 1854, p. 180) Customarily, the entire family accompanied the men to the national celebrations in well-equipped caravans. Accordingly, Luke comments that both Joseph and Mary "went to Jerusalem *every* year at the Feast of the Passover."[407]

When Joseph, Mary, and twelve-year-old Jesus made the trip to Jerusalem to attend the annual Passover celebration, they traveled in a caravan.[408] At the conclusion of the Passover festivity, Jesus' parents inadvertently left Him behind in Jerusalem as their caravan departed for Nazareth, a caravan so large that they "went a day's journey" before discovering none of their "relatives and acquaintances" had Jesus.[409] Having realized their oversight, Joseph and Mary returned to Jerusalem, consuming a second day.[410] Upon arriving in Jerusalem, "after three days they found Him in the Temple, sitting in the midst of the teachers, both

---

[404] Matthew 2:10 BT
[405] Matthew 2:9 BT
[406] Deuteronomy 16:16; Exodus 23:14-17; 34:18-24
[407] Luke 2:41-42 NASU
[408] Luke 2:44 NASU
[409] Luke 2:44 NASU
[410] Luke 2:45

listening to them and asking them questions."[411] They had misplaced Jesus for five days.

In the same manner as they traveled to the annual festivals in Jerusalem, Joseph and Mary would have journeyed to Bethlehem in a family caravan to register in the Roman census. With them would have traveled their fathers (Jacob and Eli), mothers, siblings, grandfather (Matthan), other Nazarene[412] relatives who descended from David, and any relatives who may have joined them along the way. As Luke explained, "*Everyone* was on his way to register for the census, each to his own city" of ancestry.[413]

Descendants of King David who had come from everywhere to register would have crowded into Bethlehem. Although Joseph had planned to lodge at the Bethlehem inn, he found no vacancy due to the multitude of visitors.[414] He likely resorted to setting up the tent[415] he would have pitched each night as the caravan traveled from Nazareth to Bethlehem, a journey of about a week.

The Animal Lot

Sometime after their arrival at Bethlehem, Mary gave birth to Jesus.[416] Her use of a feeding trough as a crib[417] indicates the caravan located in an area frequented by domestic animals, for *no* member of the caravan would have found room at the inn. The animal trough protected Jesus from the movement of others around Him. Had Mary placed Him on the tent floor, people could have accidently injured Him. Considering stone animal troughs remained virtually immobile, Joseph probably pitched his

---

[411] Contrary to traditional legend, Joseph and Mary did not find twelve-year-old Jesus in the Temple teaching the teachers, but "sitting in the midst of the teachers, both listening to them and asking questions" (Luke 2:46 NASU). For additional information regarding this episode, see "Appendix 1: 12-Year-Old Jesus in Temple."

[412] Nazarene – a person from the town of Nazareth

[413] Luke 2:3 NASU

[414] Luke 2:7

[415] The apostle Paul, Aquila, and Priscilla would have manufactured similar caravan tents when practicing their occupational trade (Acts 18:3).

[416] Luke 2:6

[417] Luke 2:7

tent next to the weighty manger.[418]

Stone, abundant and inexpensive, served as the primary construction material in the region. Forests did not grow in the Bethlehem area. Thickets thrived far away along the Jordan River but did not supply material for production of goods. Only the wealthy could afford craft-quality lumber, an expensive luxury imported from distant lands such as the hills of Lebanon.[419] Hence, craftsmen[420] utilized stone to make everything from buildings,[421] city walls,[422] and houses,[423] to water pots,[424] millstones,[425] and animal troughs.[426]

Ancient Stone Trough Located in an Open Area at Megiddo, Israel

Figure 5 - 1 (www.HolyLandPhotos.org)

---

[418] Early writers of English, 14th century and later, referred to an animal trough as a manger.

[419] 1 Kings 5:6; 2 Chronicles 2:9-11

[420] For additional information about the craftsmen of that day, see "Chapter 3 – Birth of Jesus, Rescuer of His People," heading "Joseph (Matthew 1:18)," subheading "Joseph the Craftsman."

[421] Mark 13:1-2; Luke 21:5-6

[422] Revelation 21:14,19; Luke 19:43-44

[423] 1 Peter 2:4-5

[424] John 2:6

[425] Matthew 18:6; Mark 9:42; Luke 17:2

[426] Luke 2:7,12,16

The Shepherds

The night of Mary's delivery, one of God's angels announced the birth of the Messiah to shepherds in the fields outside Bethlehem. They hurried into the village in search of the infant. Upon finding Him, the shepherds explained to Joseph and Mary that the angel identified this Child as indeed the Messiah.[427]

Shepherds' Fields (About 1919 A.D.)

Figure 5 - 2

Shepherds' Fields at Night (About 1919 A.D.)

Figure 5 - 3

---

[427] Luke 2:8-20; For a discussion of the meaning of "Messiah" and "Christ," see "Chapter 2 – Kings & Scoundrels: Jesus' Ancestors," heading "The One Called Christ (Matthew 1:1, 16-17)."

The House

Although the caravan camped in an animal lot, the Magi found Jesus elsewhere. By the time the star "stood above where the Child was," Joseph had found accommodations more suitable. The Magi found his family lodging in a house.[428]

What About the Stable?

The origin of the traditional story that Mary gave birth to Jesus in the stable of the Bethlehem inn has proven elusive. No one has offered credible historical evidence to support that assertion. Moreover, the circumstances surrounding Jesus' birth show the unlikelihood of the stable legend.

John Kitto thoroughly explored Palestine in 1838 and again in 1852. As part of his research, Dr. Kitto became familiar with numerous inns of the region, typically called khans[429] or caravansaries.[430] He commented, "Many caravanserais,[431] however, have not the accommodation of stables, the cattle being allowed to range in the open area." (Kitto, 1846, p. 397)

Caravansary Ruins at Aphek, Ancient Judean City (1932 A.D.)

Figure 5 - 4

---

[428] Matthew 2:11

[429] Khan (kän)

[430] Caravansary (kâr-ə-vǎn-sə-rē)

[431] Caravanserais – Dr. Kitto's antiquated spelling of caravansaries

Small-town inns offered guests only a tiny room with a dirt floor and the light entering through the doorway. In contrast, some *city* caravansaries offered stables, stone-paved floors, servants, food, cooks, sale of goods, and other conveniences. Dr. Kitto observed, "Caravanserais of this superior class, however, are rarely met with." (Kitto, 1846, p. 395) The small-town inn of Bethlehem would not likely have had a stable.[432]

The absence of historical verification discredits the stable tradition. Furthermore, to maintain the legend one must embrace four precarious speculations.

1. The small-town inn of Bethlehem had a stable.
2. Caravan travelers lodged in the stable when the inn had no vacancy.
3. Joseph and Mary arrived at the occupied inn before other travelers filled the stable.
4. Joseph and Mary would have chosen to stay in a stinky, manure-littered stable instead of sensibly remaining with other family members in the familiar comfort of their caravan tent pitched in an open area.

The collective assumptions listed above confirm the improbability of the stable legend.

---

[432] For a discussion of the small size of Bethlehem, see "Chapter 6 – The Great Escape," heading "From Two Years and Under (Matthew 2:16)," subheading "Number of Boys Killed."

What About the Cave?

Like the stable tradition, the legend that Mary gave birth to Jesus in a cave lacks historical foundation. Its origin lies in the apocryphal[433] *Gospel of James*, as well as the writings of Justin Martyr and Origen of Alexandria.

Gospel of James

The myth-filled *Gospel of James*, composed about 145 A.D. by an unknown writer, appears chronologically as the original source of the cave legend.[434] It fraudulently attributes its authorship to James, half-brother of Jesus, and feigns events that occurred during Jesus' infancy, clashing with the accounts of Matthew and Luke concerning circumstances surrounding Jesus' birth. Consider the following quote from the *Gospel of James*.

> *And he* [Joseph] *found there a cave, and let her* [Mary] *into it. And leaving her ... in the cave, Joseph went forth to seek a Hebrew midwife in the village of Bethlehem. ... She replied to me* [Joseph], *Where is the woman that is to be delivered? And I answered, In the cave, and she is betrothed to me. ... Then said the midwife, Is she not thy wife? Joseph answered, It is Mary, who was educated in the Holy of Holies, in the house of the Lord, and ... there arose a great disorder in Bethlehem by the coming of some wise men* [Magi] *from the east, Who said, Where is the king of the Jews born? For we have seen his star in the east, and are come to worship him. ... So the wise men went forth, and behold, the star which they saw in the east went before them, till it came and stood over the cave where the young child was with Mary his mother.*[435] (Hone, 1820, pp. 33-35)

The *Gospel of James* contradicts Matthew's account of the Magi's arrival. Matthew explained that the Magi found the young couple and their Child in a *house*, not a cave.[436] Furthermore, the Magi arrived in Bethlehem

---

[433] *Apocryphal* refers to literature, stories, or quotes of doubtful authenticity.

[434] Gospel of James 18:1

[435] *The Protevangelion* (a.k.a., *The Gospel of James*) 12:14; 13:1; 14:3-5; 15:1-2,9

[436] Matthew 2:11

at least six weeks after Jesus' birth, not the day of His birth.[437] The inaccuracies in the *Gospel of James* account of Jesus' birth discredit its claim that Mary gave birth in a cave.

Justin Martyr

Justin, born into a pagan family[438] in the city of Flavia Neapolis some 39 miles[439] north of Jerusalem, discussed Jesus' birth in his book, *Dialogue with Trypho*. About 160 A.D. he wrote,

> *The child was born at Bethlehem; and Joseph, because he could find no place in the town where to lodge, went into a certain cave near the town. And while they were there, Mary brought forth Christ, and laid him in a manger; where he was found by the wise men that came from Arabia.* (Martyr, 1755, pp. 20-21)

Justin's account conflicts with Matthew's description of the Magi's arrival. Matthew stated that, "Upon entering the house, they saw the Child with Mary, His mother."[440] They found Jesus in a *house*, not a cave. Furthermore, the Magi did not arrive in Bethlehem the day of Jesus' birth, but at least six weeks later.[441] Moreover, the Magi lived within the Parthian Empire, not Arabia.[442] The inaccuracies in Justin's account of Jesus' birth, a repetition of the myth invented by the writer of the *Gospel of James*, render unreliable his statement that Mary gave birth in a cave.

---

[437] For a discussion of the period within which the Magi arrived in Bethlehem, see "Chapter 5 – The Magi Meet Jesus, King of the Jews," heading "The Star Stood Above Where the Child Was (Matthew 2:9)," subheading "When Did the Magi Arrive in Bethlehem?"

[438] Justin Martyr became a Christian during his adult years.

[439] 63 kilometers

[440] Matthew 2:11 BT

[441] For a discussion of the period within which the Magi arrived in Bethlehem, see "Chapter 5 – The Magi Meet Jesus, King of the Jews," heading "The Star Stood Above Where the Child Was (Matthew 2:9)," subheading "When Did the Magi Arrive in Bethlehem?"

[442] For a discussion of the homeland of the Magi, see "Chapter 4 – The Magi Meet Herod, King of Judea," heading "Magi from the East (Matthew 2:1)."

Origen of Alexandria

Origen, born in Alexandria, Egypt to Christian parents, touched on the birth of Jesus in his book, *Against Celsus*. About 248 A.D. he wrote,

> *With respect to the birth of Jesus in Bethlehem, ... there is shown at Bethlehem the cave where He was born, and the manger in the cave where He was wrapped in swaddling-clothes. And this sight is greatly talked of in surrounding places, even among the enemies of the faith, **it being said** that in this cave was born that Jesus who is worshipped and reverenced by the Christians.* (Origen, 1869, p. 453)

Origen reported rumor when he wrote, "*it being said* that in this cave was born ... Jesus." He never claimed to have seen the cave himself, nor did he imply that anyone should accept such hearsay as historical evidence. He merely documented the existence of the legend.

The cave tradition relies solely on the statements of the *Gospel of James*, Justin Martyr, and Origen of Alexandria, which provide no historical credibility for the legend. Furthermore, to maintain the tradition one must embrace the irrational assumption that Joseph and Mary would have chosen to stay in a dirty, damp cave instead of with other family members in the relative comfort of their caravan tent.[443] The absence of historical foundation and lack of motive for Joseph and Mary to have lodged in a cave prove the cave legend untrustworthy.

---

[443] For a discussion of the family caravan in which Joseph and Mary would have traveled to Bethlehem, see "Chapter 5 – The Magi Meet Jesus, King of the Jews," heading "The Star Stood Above Where the Child Was (Matthew 2:9)," subheading "The Caravan."

***

Contemplation Points

1. How many Magi visited Jesus?
    a. Do you know of a Scripture that mentions the number?
    b. Do you know of any *credible historical* source stating the number?
    c. How does one distinguish between truth and myth?
    d. What myth relates to the number of Magi who visited Jesus?
2. Where did the Magi find Jesus and His parents? (Read Matthew 2:11.)
    a. Where does the *traditional* nativity scene place them when the Magi arrived?
    b. Can one rely on the traditions of men to be true?
        i. If so, explain why.
        ii. If not, explain why not.
    c. How can one distinguish between truth and the traditions of men?

Date of Jesus' Birth

Each year, many Christians observe December 25 as Jesus' birthday. Yet, the Scriptures do not divulge the date of Jesus' birth, nor does God direct an annual celebration of that day. Since this tradition did not originate with God, from where did it come?

In 221 A.D., Sextus Julius Africanus convinced himself through speculative analysis that God created Earth on March 25, the spring equinox. Building on that arbitrary date, he declared Mary must have also conceived Jesus on March 25, the day of new beginnings.[444]

In 274 A.D., the Roman emperor Aurelian established December 25 as a public holiday to celebrate the birth of Mithras, Rome's sun god. In 336 A.D., a group of Christians in Rome first celebrated the birth of Jesus on December 25, choosing that date to counter the Roman holiday. So

---

[444] *Chronographia*, Sextus Julius Africanus' history of the world from creation to 221 A.D.

began the tradition of what eight centuries later came to be called Christmas (i.e., Christ's mass).

In 525 A.D., Dionysius Exiguus[445] accepted as fact Africanus' supposition that Mary conceived Jesus on March 25. Further assuming that Mary must have completed an exact nine-month pregnancy, Exiguus proclaimed Jesus' birth to have occurred on December 25. Ignoring the absence of credible historical evidence, Exiguus drew his conclusion based on Africanus' unsupported speculations, as well as his own irrational assumption.

Although no historical data exists to approximate the month and day of Jesus' birth, one can deduce a range for His birth year by considering two facts. First, Herod the Great died in 4 B.C.[446] Second, Herod murdered all boys in the Bethlehem area "two years and under," confident the birth of the Child he sought took place within the previous two years.[447] Subtracting two years from the year Herod died, logic dictates that Jesus' birth happened within the span of 6-4 B.C.

***

Contemplation Point

- Do you celebrate the birthday of Jesus?
  - o If so, explain why.
  - o If not, explain why not.

When Did the Magi Arrive in Bethlehem?

The Magi arrived in Bethlehem between six weeks and two years after Jesus' birth. *Six weeks* passed after His birth before Mary offered the required animal sacrifices related to the delivery of a baby. Herod chose the age-range of *two years* and under for the boys he would kill. An analysis of both periods reveals the window of time in which the Magi appeared at Joseph's doorstep.

---

[445] Dionysius Exiguus (dī-ŭ-nĭ-shē-ŭs ĕg-zĭ-gyū-wŭs), a Roman Catholic monk
[446] For a calculation of the date Herod died, see "Chapter 4 – The Magi Meet Herod, King of Judea," heading "Herod's Death."
[447] Matthew 2:7,16 BT

Six-Week Time Period

God required Israelite parents of a male infant to circumcise him on the eighth day after birth.[448] Joseph and Mary faithfully fulfilled that obligation.[449] Following the circumcision, another 33 days had to pass *completely* prior to the mother's provision of two designated animals to the priest for sacrifice.[450] Luke refers to that 33-day period as "the days of their purification."[451]

God's Covenant with Israel instructed a new mother to provide two sacrificial animals to the priest at the Temple in Jerusalem upon the full completion of 41 days after the birth of a son (8+33=41). The animals served as a "burnt offering" and a "sin offering."[452] For the burnt offering God required a one-year-old lamb and for the sin offering a young pigeon or a turtledove. He allowed the mother to substitute a turtledove or a young pigeon if she did not have sufficient resources to offer a lamb for the burnt offering.[453]

Lacking the funds to buy a lamb, Mary offered two birds on the 42nd day following Jesus' birth, one for the burnt offering and one for the sin offering.[454] Since she did not have the money to purchase a lamb, she and Joseph did not yet possess the treasures[455] the Magi would bring to their Child. Hence, six weeks (42 days)[456] into the earthly life of Jesus, the Magi had not yet arrived in Bethlehem.

The old Covenant between God and Israel, under which Mary gave birth to Jesus, allowed few rights for children. Parents had almost unlimited power over their offspring, exercising life and death control.[457] Children,

---

[448] Leviticus 12:1-8
[449] Luke 2:21
[450] Leviticus 12:1-8
[451] Luke 2:22 NASU
[452] Leviticus 12:1-8
[453] Leviticus 12:1-8
[454] Luke 2:24
[455] Matthew 2:11
[456] 7 full days before circumcision + 1 day for the circumcision + 33 full days of purification + 1 day for the sacrifices = 42 days; 42 days ÷ 7 days = 6 weeks
[457] Exodus 21:15,17; Deuteronomy 21:18-21

considered the property of their parents, had no legal possessions. Parents could sell a child as a slave, and creditors could seize a child as payment of a debt the parents had failed to pay.[458] Although the Magi presented their treasures to the child Jesus, the gifts would have remained the legal property of His parents, Joseph and Mary.

Joseph did not live impoverished. His trade paid a living wage,[459] and his earnings later provided for his wife and children.[460] He came to Bethlehem prepared to pay for lodging at the inn. Furthermore, Joseph had resources to travel each year to the Passover celebration in Jerusalem,[461] and as a devout man he would have attended the other two annual religious festivals in Jerusalem as well, the Pentecost and the Feast of Booths.[462]

Since Joseph earned a decent livelihood, why could Mary not afford a sacrificial lamb? They had likely anticipated Jesus' birth to take place after their return to Nazareth. Their decision not to go back to Nazareth with the caravan averted traveling with a newborn and avoided the necessity of a return trip to Jerusalem six weeks later to offer the required sacrifices. The additional expense of their extended stay in Bethlehem would have strained the couple's budget. When the day came for Mary to provide the priest two animals for sacrifice, insufficient funds remained to purchase a lamb.

***

Contemplation Points

1. How seriously would weeks of extended layover strain *your* travel budget?
2. What challenges would you face?
3. What challenges would Joseph and Mary have faced?

---

[458] Exodus 21:7; 2 Kings 4:1

[459] For information concerning Joseph's trade, see "Chapter 3 – Birth of Jesus, Rescuer of His People, heading Joseph (Matthew 1:18)," subheading "Joseph the Craftsman." For information regarding his employment opportunities in nearby Sepphoris, see "Chapter 7 – Going Home," heading "He Resided in Nazareth (Matthew 2:23)," subheading "Nazareth (Matthew 2:23)."

[460] Matthew 12:46; 13:53-56; Mark 6:1-4; Luke 8:19-21; John 2:12; 1 Corinthians 9:5

[461] Luke 2:41

[462] Deuteronomy 16:16; Exodus 23:14-17; 34:18-24

Two-Year Time Period

Herod, certain he could eliminate the Child sought by the Magi, ordered the murder of all boys in the Bethlehem area "two years and under."[463] He determined the Child had not reached His second birthday according to the precise date the star had appeared to the Magi.[464]

Given the two time constraints, undeniably the Magi arrived in Bethlehem between six weeks and two years following the birth of Jesus.

Timeline to Magi's Arrival in Bethlehem

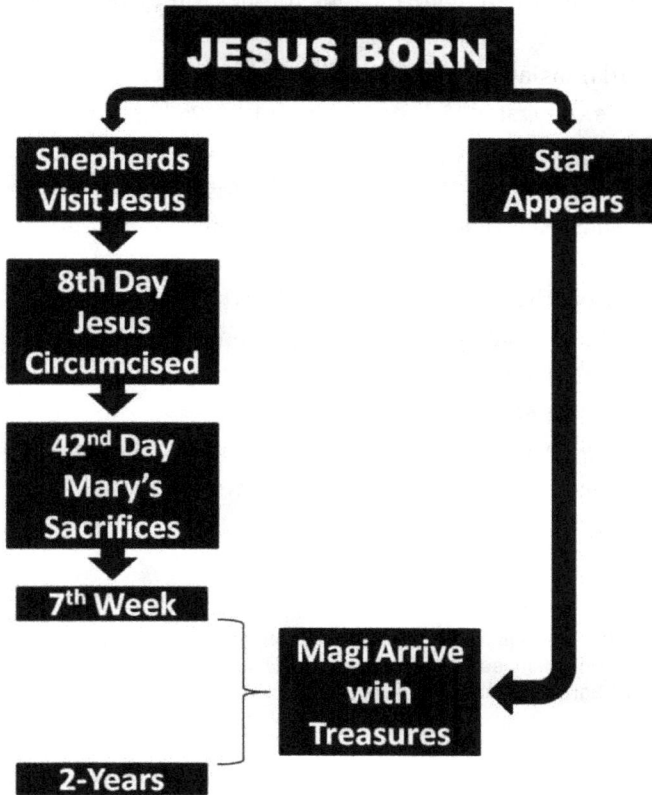

Figure 5 - 5

---

[463] Matthew 2:16 BT
[464] Matthew 2:7

They Worshiped Him (Matthew 2:11)

The procession of Magi and Parthian[465] military escort departed southward from Jerusalem on the road to Bethlehem, following the re-emerged star.

Upon arriving at the house in which Joseph, Mary, and Jesus stayed, the Magi would have modestly requested permission to enter the home. Imagine their gaze of admiration and awe as they caught sight of the Child. Remembering why they had made the long journey, "they fell down and *worshiped* Him."[466]

The Greek word translated "worshiped," *prosekúnesan* (prŏs-ĕ-kú-nā-sän),[467] appears as a conjugated[468] form of the infinitive[469] *proskunéo* (prŏs-kü-nḗ-ō).[470] The word *proskunéo* divides into two parts. *Pros* (prŏs),[471] the first part, means "toward." *Kunéo* (kü-nḗ-ō),[472] the second part, means "to kiss" as in a kiss of submission, not a brotherly or intimate kiss.

Kunéo derived from the word *kúon* (kú-ōn),[473] which means "dog." It depicts the humility of a crouching dog as it shyly approaches its master. Timidly licking in the air, the dog's tongue eventually makes lowly contact with its master's extended hand.

Although *proskunéo* developed from such imagery, the ancient Greeks came to apply the word to any expression of worship, especially

---

[465] For information regarding the relationship of the Magi to the Parthian Empire, see "Chapter 4 – The Magi Meet Herod, King of Judea," heading "His Star (Matthew 2:2)," subheading "Parthian Empire and the Magi" and subheading "Magi Arrive in Jerusalem."

[466] Matthew 2:11 BT

[467] *Prosekúnesan* (prŏs-ĕ-kú-nā-sän), προσεκύνησαν

[468] Conjugated – A conjugated form of an infinitive reflects the number, person, tense, etc. that a writer intends to communicate.

[469] Infinitive – a verb form with no indication of person, number, mood, or tense (Examples of infinitives include *to eat, to run*, and *to swim.*)

[470] *Proskunéo* (prŏs-kü-nḗ-ō), προσκυνέω

[471] *Pros* (prŏs), προσ

[472] *Kunéo* (kü-nḗ-ō), κυνέω

[473] *Kúon* (kú-ōn), κύων

prostration.[474] Of the 60 times New Testament writers employ various grammatical forms of *proskunéo*, 15 times an act of prostration accompanies it.[475] In this unassuming manner, the Magi lowered themselves to the ground showing reverence and honor, acknowledging the superiority of the divine Child.[476]

***

Contemplation Points

1. Describe the attitude you maintain when worshiping the Lord.
2. Do you ever assume a particular posture while worshiping?
   a. If so, what kind?
   b. Why?
3. How does the attitude of your worship compare with that of the Magi?

They Offered Him Gifts (Matthew 2:11)

Once the Magi rose from the ground, "they opened their treasures and offered Him gifts of gold and frankincense and myrrh."[477] Although the Scriptures do not specify the amount of each item, certainly the gifts carried extreme value for Matthew called them "treasures."

In ancient times, when a king granted an audience to a visitor, the guest customarily brought gifts of treasure to honor the royalty. For example, when the Queen of Sheba visited Solomon, King of Israel,

> *She came to Jerusalem with a very large retinue, with camels carrying spices[478] and very much gold and precious stones. ... She*

---

[474] Prostration – kneeling on both knees with one's face touching the ground or lying flat with one's face on the ground
[475] Matthew 2:11; 4:9; 18:26; 28:9; Mark 15:19; Acts 10:25; 1 Corinthians 14:25; Revelation 3:9; 4:10; 5:14; 7:11; 11:16; 19:4,10; 22:8
[476] See also Genesis 24: 26;48; Exodus 4:31; 12:27; 2 Chronicles 29:29-30; Nehemiah 8:6; Job 1:20; Psalm 2:11; 5:7; Matthew 28:9; Revelation 5:14; 7:11; 11:16; 19:4.
[477] Matthew 2:11 BT
[478] Frankincense and myrrh – among the many precious spices cherished in the distant past

> *gave the king a hundred and twenty talents[479] of gold, and a very great amount of spices and precious stones.*[480]

The Magi, like the Queen of Sheba, would have shared a generous portion of their treasure as an integral part of their homage to Jesus, King of the Jews. Bear in mind, they made their long journey specifically "to worship Him."[481]

***

Contemplation Points

1. How do your gifts to God compare to those of the Magi?
2. Over your lifetime, will the total of your gifts express the same reverent worship as the Magi?
   a. If so, explain how.
   b. If not, explain why not.

What Is Frankincense?

Value of Frankincense

The Magi's gifts consisted of gold, frankincense, and myrrh – all of great worth. Frankincense, the most cherished, brought a price more than its weight in gold due to its remote foreign origin, limited availability, and numerous applications. The Magi's decision to include frankincense among the "treasures"[482] their caravan would haul to Judea reflected the magnitude of honor they planned to lavish upon "the one who has been born King of the Jews."[483]

Herodotus, a Greek historian who lived during the fifth century B.C., provided an example of the enormous worth of frankincense in his day. He recorded that the Arabs gave Darius the Great, King of the Persian

---

[479] Talent – a standard measure referring to a weight of silver equal to about 93¾ pounds (42.5 kilograms) [A gold talent weighed twice that of a silver talent. For a brow-raiser, use today's price of gold to calculate the value of 120 talents in your currency (120 gold talents ≈ 187,500 pounds ≈ 85,000 kilograms).]

[480] 1 Kings 10:1-2,10 NASU

[481] Matthew 2:2 BT

[482] Matthew 2:11 BT

[483] Matthew 2:2 BT

Empire,[484] 1,000 talents of frankincense as payment of their annual tribute[485] to him. (Herodotus, 1848, p. 213)[486] That amount of frankincense would have been of more value than 93,750 pounds[487] of silver.

Frankincense Trees

Frankincense, a gummy resin also called *olibanum,*[488] comes from various leafy trees in the *Boswellia*[489] genus. The Boswellia genus contains at least 25 species of frankincense trees. Some varieties of the frankincense tree grow only a few feet tall, while others reach twenty feet in height. It has silvery-colored bark and prickly branches. These trees thrive in the lime-rich soil of dry riverbeds, hillsides, and rocky cliffs.

Frankincense Harvest

When harvesting frankincense, a *cutter* makes deep incisions in the tree's limbs, out of which a sticky, milk-colored sap begins to seep. Over a period of three weeks, the exposed sap hardens into large, semitransparent *tears*. Once the sap dries, a harvester scrapes off the solid, tear-shaped lumps of yellowish resin and gathers them into containers.

---

[484] Darius ruled the Persian Empire 521-486 B.C.

[485] Tribute, a payment by a weaker nation to a stronger nation, demonstrated submission to the superior nation in exchange for the superior nation's promise not to invade.

[486] *The Histories of Herodotus*, Book 3, Paragraph 97

[487] Talent – a standard measure referring to a weight of silver equal to about 93¾ pounds (42.5 kilograms) [A gold talent weighed twice that of a silver talent. For a brow-raiser, use today's price of silver to calculate the value of 1,000 talents in your currency (1000 silver talents ≈ 93,750 pounds ≈ 42,500 kilograms).]

[488] *Olibanum* (ō-lĭb-ə-nŭm)

[489] *Boswellia* (bŏs-wĕl-lē-ə)

Frankincense Regions

Frankincense trees grow in southwest Asia, within the southern region of the Arabian Peninsula. They also grow in the dry areas of the northeast coast of Africa, not far south of the Arabian Peninsula. The frankincense of the Magi originated from those areas.

Map: Frankincense Regions

Figure 5 - 6

Uses of Frankincense

Widely utilized as incense, a globule of frankincense placed directly on top of burning coals yielded a fragrant aroma. God commanded the priests of Israel to include this sweet-smelling spice among the ingredients mixed with the incense burned in the Tabernacle.[490] In later

[490] Exodus 30:34-38

centuries, priests employed that same mixture in the Jerusalem Temple.

When distilled, frankincense resin yields a volatile oil. Makers of perfumes, lotions, creams, and soaps blended in frankincense oil with their other ingredients.[491] Frankincense also served as a natural insecticide and insect repellant.

Early Greeks and Romans utilized frankincense in various potions to treat a broad range of ailments. Muslim, Syrian, Indian, and Chinese writings mention it as an ingredient in assorted medicinal preparations. Physicians applied it topically to inflamed areas to reduce swelling. Taken internally, it eased intestinal blockage. When chewed, it reduced coughing and prevented bad breath. In addition, frankincense relieved irritated eyes when mixed with eyewashes.

What Is Myrrh?

Value of Myrrh

Myrrh ranked close to frankincense in value, though a little less costly. Like frankincense, it rivaled the price of gold as one of the most expensive commodities in the ancient world due to its remote foreign origin, limited availability, and numerous applications. The Magi chose well to place myrrh among the "treasures"[492] they brought to the "King of the Jews."[493]

Myrrh Trees

Myrrh, an aromatic gum resin, comes from various thorny shrubs of the *Commiphora*[494] genus. The Commiphora genus contains over 60 species of scraggly shrubs, sometimes referred to as *diddin* trees. Some varieties grow to be only a few feet tall, while others reach nine feet.

---

[491] Song of Solomon 3:6-11
[492] Matthew 2:11 BT
[493] Matthew 2:2 BT
[494] *Commiphora* (cŏm-mĭ-phō-rə)

Harvesting Myrrh

When harvesting myrrh, a *cutter* makes deep gashes into the limbs of the shrubs to allow resin to seep from beneath the bark. A pale-yellow secretion oozes from each incision. It takes two weeks for the exposed sap to harden into solid globules about the size of walnuts, ranging in color from yellowish brown to reddish brown. Scraping the brittle lumps off the tree, a harvester gathers them into containers.

Myrrh Regions

Myrrh trees grow in arid, rocky, barren hill country. Like frankincense, myrrh shrubs are native to southwest Asia, within the southern region of the Arabian Peninsula. They also thrive in the dry areas of the northeast coast of Africa, not far south of the Arabian Peninsula. The myrrh of the Magi originated from those areas.

Map: Myrrh Regions

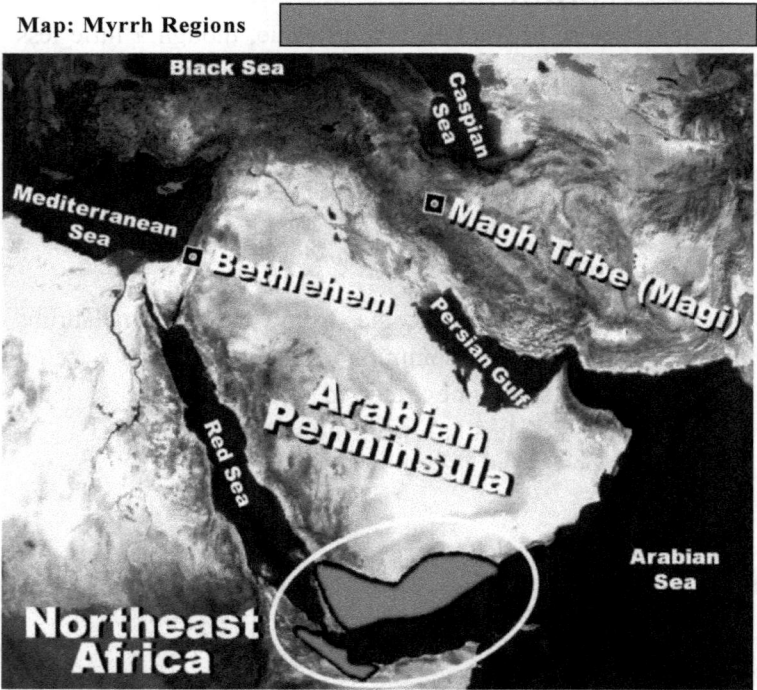

Figure 5 - 7

Uses of Myrrh

Ancient civilizations burned myrrh as incense. They also added it to perfumes. God commanded the priests of Israel to include myrrh among the ingredients mixed into the "holy anointing oil."[495]

Like frankincense, myrrh had an extensive list of ancient medicinal benefits. Physicians mixed it with topical ointments to heal wounds. Myrrh suppressed bleeding and aided in the extraction of foreign material from an open wound.

The ancients also consumed myrrh as a recreational drug. It induced a drowsy, trance-like stupor when swallowed. Romans mixed it with wine to increase the intoxicating effect of alcohol.

While Jesus hung on the cross, His executioners offered Him wine mixed with *gall*,[496] a generic word referring to the extract from several kinds of plants. Mark identified the gall mixed with the wine given to Jesus as myrrh.[497] Jesus "refused to drink it."[498]

Review of Matthew's Text (Matthew 2:9-12)

> *9 Having heeded the king, they traveled on their way. And look, the star that they saw in the east led the way before them until it stood above where the Child was. 10 They rejoiced with exceedingly great joy when they saw the star. 11 Upon entering the house, they saw the Child with Mary, His mother. After they fell down and worshipped Him, they opened their treasures and offered Him gifts of gold and frankincense and myrrh. 12 Then, having been warned in a dream not to return to Herod, they departed by another way to their own country.* (BT)

---

[495] Exodus 30:22-23

[496] Matthew 27:34

[497] Mark 15:23

[498] Matthew 27:34 BT; Take care not to confuse the wine-gall mixture with the vinegar-soaked sponge mentioned in Matthew 27:48.

....

CHAPTER 6

The Great Escape

The Magi found the One born King of the Jews, worshiped Him, and honored Him with exotic treasures. They then turned their caravan homeward and "having been warned in a dream not to return to Herod, they departed by another way to their own country."[499]

Matthew's Text (Matthew 2:13-18)[500]

13 After they departed, listen up, an angel of the Lord appeared to Joseph in a dream, saying, "Arise, take the Child and His mother and flee into Egypt. Stay there until I tell you, because Herod is about to search for the Child to destroy Him."

14 Then, after getting up, he took the Child and His mother and departed by night into Egypt. 15 Now, he stayed there until Herod's death, that the thing spoken by the Lord through Hosea might be fulfilled, saying, "Out of Egypt I called My Son."

---

[499] Matthew 2:12 BT
[500] No passages within the books of Mark, Luke, or John parallel Matthew 2:13-18.

16 Then Herod, seeing that he had been made a fool of by the Magi, became very angry. Consequently, based on the exact time he had learned from the Magi, he sent out an order to kill all the boys from two years and under in Bethlehem and the surrounding area.

17 Then the word spoken through the prophet Jeremiah was fulfilled, saying, 18 "A sound of much crying and lamenting was heard in Ramah — Rachel, crying over her children, and she did not want to be comforted because they are no more." (BT)

Flight into Egypt (Matthew 2:13-14)

Run for Your Life

Herod realized the Magi had ignored his instruction to advise him of the Child's location, so he designed another plan to find and kill Jesus. Meanwhile, sleeping, Joseph received a warning from an angel to escape to Egypt with his family. Aware that Herod's soldiers had only a five-mile[501] ride southward from Jerusalem to Bethlehem, Joseph immediately rose from bed and hastily threw together provisions. Sneaking away into the night, he navigated southwestward toward Egypt, taking Mary and Jesus out of harm's way.

---

[501] Eight-kilometer

Jerusalem to Bethlehem (1931 A.D.)

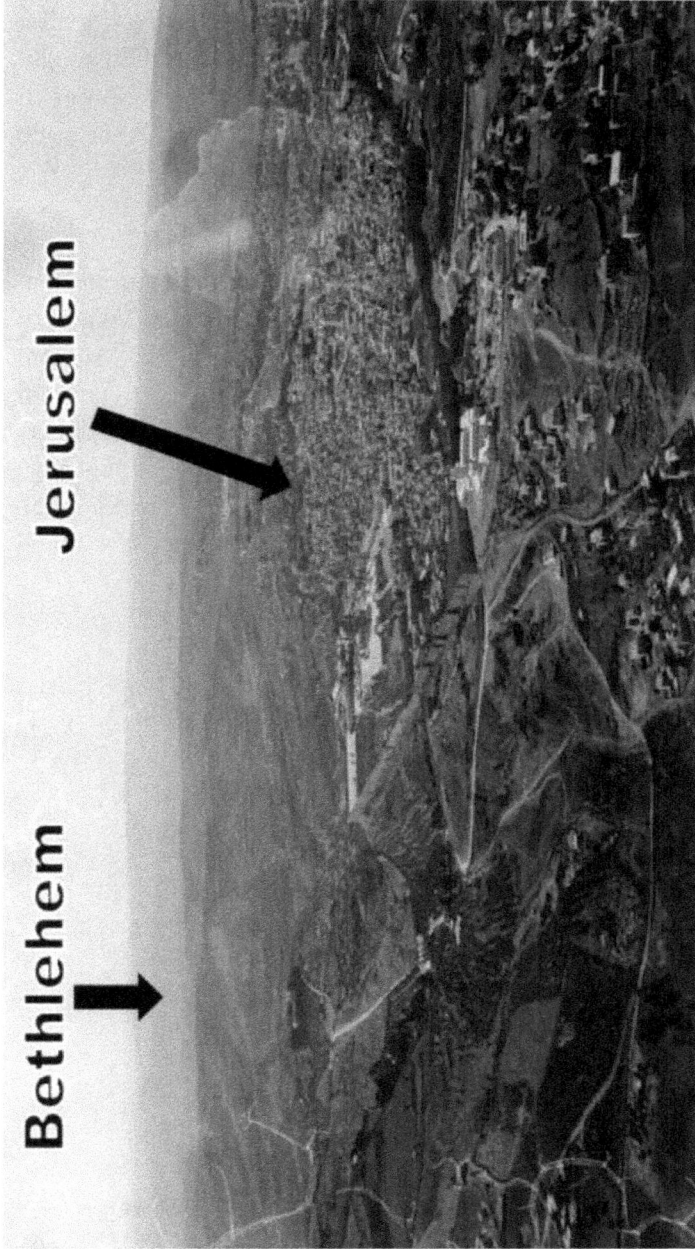

Figure 6 - 1

119

The soldiers came to Bethlehem with orders to murder all boys in the area aged "two years and under."[502] As they took one young life after another, Herod felt assured his soldiers would terminate the Child sought by the Magi. Nonetheless, Joseph evaded Herod's henchmen. No one in Bethlehem knew to point the soldiers toward Egypt. Even so, what made Egypt a place of safety?

Out of Herod's Reach

Joseph traveled a week or more before reaching the Judean-Egyptian border, about 110 miles[503] from Bethlehem. The Wadi of Egypt,[504] nothing more than a dry riverbed except during the rainy season, served as the boundary separating the Roman province of Egypt from Rome's client kingdom[505] of Judea ruled by Herod. Had Herod's soldiers crossed the Wadi while searching for the Child, they and Herod would have had to answer to Caesar Augustus for their infringement into Egyptian territory. Since Herod's legal jurisdiction ended at the border, Joseph found safe haven in Egypt.

---

[502] Matthew 2:16 BT

[503] 177 kilometers

[504] Writers also refer to the Wadi of Egypt as the Wadi el-'Arish and the Brook of Egypt.

[505] Client kingdom – a kingdom economically, politically, and militarily subordinate to another ruling power. (A client kingdom of Rome possessed a lower political status than a Roman province.)

Map: Escape to Egypt

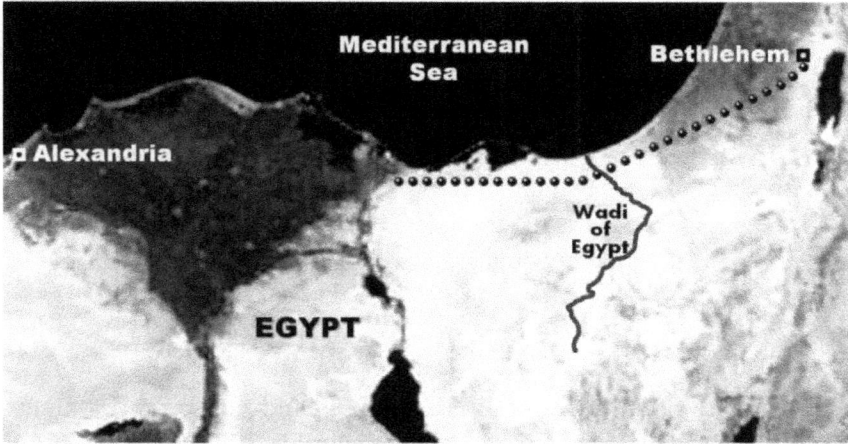

Figure 6 - 2

***

Contemplation Points

1. Have you ever had to flee from your home for an extended period?
    a. If so, what concerned you?
    b. How did you cope?
2. What would have concerned Joseph and Mary
    a. During their race to Egypt?
    b. While they remained in Egypt?
3. How might they have coped?

Support System

By God's provision through the treasures of the Magi, Joseph had abundant funding for relocation and settlement in a foreign land. Although Matthew did not mention the region of Egypt in which Joseph and Mary sojourned, they likely found their way to one of the several Jewish colonies that had developed within Egypt over the centuries. For example, some scholars estimate several hundred thousand Jews lived in Alexandria, a major city on the northern Mediterranean coast of Egypt, a three-week,

350-mile[506] journey from Bethlehem. In such a colony, Joseph's family would have found a support system in which they could live without fear.

From Two Years and Under (Matthew 2:16)

Joseph and Mary had no idea of the horror about to take place as they slipped out of town that night. Herod employed every means to ensure that no one threatened his rule over Judea. His obsession for power led him to order the massacre of "all the boys from two years and under in Bethlehem and the surrounding area."[507]

Counting Age

The Jews did not speak of the age of a child as one, two, or three years old. Instead, they spoke of a child living his "first year," "second year," "third year," and so on. A child in his "first year" had not yet reached his first birthday, and a child in his "second year" had not reached his second birthday. Therefore, when Herod declared "two years and under," he targeted boys in their first or second year of life.

Number of Boys Killed

The prophet Micah described the village of Bethlehem as "too little to be among the *clans* of Judah."[508] The Hebrew word rendered "among the clans" literally means "among the thousands." About 10 centuries before Micah, Moses divided each tribe of Israel into households numbering about 1,000 males 20 or more years old.[509] Thus, when Micah spoke of *thousands*, he had in mind clans of roughly a thousand men plus their families.

Micah, who wrote his book around 725 B.C., depicted Bethlehem as having less than the 1,000 men needed to qualify as its own clan. By the mid-19th century A.D., Bethlehem had grown to a population of around 4,000. (Miller, 1871, p. 148) For the sake of estimating the number of boys

---

[506] 563-kilometer
[507] Matthew 2:16 BT
[508] Micah 5:2 NASU
[509] Numbers 1:1-16 (Note verses 2-3 and 16.)

Herod's soldiers killed, we will assume the Bethlehem vicinity reached 2,000 by the time Mary gave birth.

Boys who have not yet reached their second birthday comprise approximately 1.2% of the world's population, based on United Nations statistics.[510] If Bethlehem and its surrounding area grew to around 2,000 by Jesus' birth, then Herod's soldiers killed perhaps 24 boys (2,000 × 1.2% = 24). As word of the massacre spread, some families may have hidden their young sons, just as Jochebed hid Moses from those sent to kill newborn Hebrew boys in Egypt.[511] Hence, the children slaughtered could have numbered fewer than 24.[512]

---

[510] The calculation of the percent of the world's population consisting of males less than two years of age comes from data provided by the Population Division of the Department of Economic and Social Affairs of the United Nations Secretariat, *World Population Prospects: The 2008 Revision*, http://esa.un.org./unpp/p2k0data.asp, August 11, 2010.

[511] Exodus 6:20; 1:15-16,22; 2:3

[512] The children of other families who had traveled to Bethlehem to register in the census faced no danger, for they would have returned to their hometowns prior to the massacre. Herod did not dispatch his soldiers until after the Magi departed from Bethlehem, six weeks or more after Joseph and Mary had first arrived. For a discussion of the period within which the Magi arrived in Bethlehem, see "Chapter 5 – The Magi Meet Jesus, King of the Jews," heading "The Star Stood Above Where the Child Was (Matthew 2:9)," subheading "When Did the Magi Arrive in Bethlehem?"

Ramah – Rachel (Matthew 2:18)

> *Then the word spoken through the prophet Jeremiah was fulfilled,[513] saying, 'A sound of much crying and lamenting was heard in Ramah — Rachel, crying over her children, and she did not want to be comforted because they are no more.'* (Matthew 2:17-18 BT)

The Scriptures mention five towns named Ramah. The Ramah near Rachel's burial site lay[514] midway between Bethel and Jerusalem, within the territory originally occupied by the tribe of Benjamin. Rachel died giving birth to Benjamin, while traveling from the town of Bethel to Bethlehem with her husband Jacob. Benjamin later became one of the tribal patriarchs of the nation of Israel. Jacob buried Rachel where she passed away, "still some distance" from Bethlehem.[515]

Map: Ramah

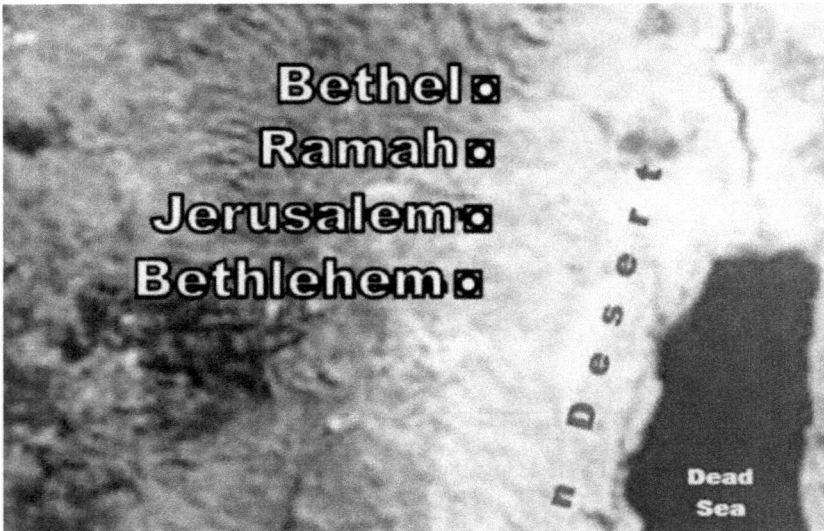

Figure 6 - 3

---

[513] Jeremiah 31:15
[514] 1 Samuel 10:2
[515] Genesis 48:7; 35:16,19

In 597 B.C., King Nebuchadnezzar[516] of Babylonia conquered the Kingdom of Judah,[517] which included the tribe of Benjamin (descendants of Rachel). Nebuchadnezzar deported tens of thousands of citizens of Judah to various regions of the Babylonian Empire.

In 539 B.C., King Cyrus of the Persian Empire conquered Babylonia[518] and allowed the exiles from Judah to return to their native soil. Members of the tribe of Judah and the tribe of Benjamin (descendants of Rachel) numbered among those who returned.[519] Those Judahites and Benjamites resettled the region surrounding Jerusalem. Within that region lay Ramah five miles north [520] of Jerusalem and Bethlehem five miles south. [521]

In Joseph and Mary's day, the original borders of the tribes of Israel no longer existed. Over centuries, a series of Gentile conquerors had divided the land into political regions whose borders did not coincide with Israel's ancestral boundaries.[522] Towns throughout those regions contained descendants of multiple Israelite tribes.

Consider Joseph and Mary as a case in point. Although both descended from the *southern* tribe of Judah, they lived in Nazareth, a town located within the territory God originally assigned to the *northern* tribe of Zebulun.

---

[516] Nebuchadnezzar (nĕb-ü-khăd-nĕz-zər)

[517] For more information about Nebuchadnezzar's conquest of the Kingdom of Judah, see Chapter 2 – Kings & Scoundrels: Jesus' Ancestors," heading "The Babylonian Deportation (Matthew 1:11)," subheading "Babylonian Deportation (of Judah)."

[518] For more information about Cyrus' conquest of the Babylonian Empire, see "Chapter 2 – Kings & Scoundrels: Jesus' Ancestors," heading "The Babylonian Deportation (Matthew 1:11)," subheading "Babylonian Deportation (of Judah)."

[519] Ezra 1:5; 4:1; 10:9

[520] Eight kilometers

[521] Eight kilometers

[522] For additional information about the Roman political divisions, see "Chapter 4 – The Magi Meet Herod, King of Judea," heading "Judea (Matthew 2:1)," subheadings "Roman Kingdom of Judea," "Roman Tetrarchy of Judea," and "Roman Province of Judea."

Map: Judah & Zebulun – Tribal Territories

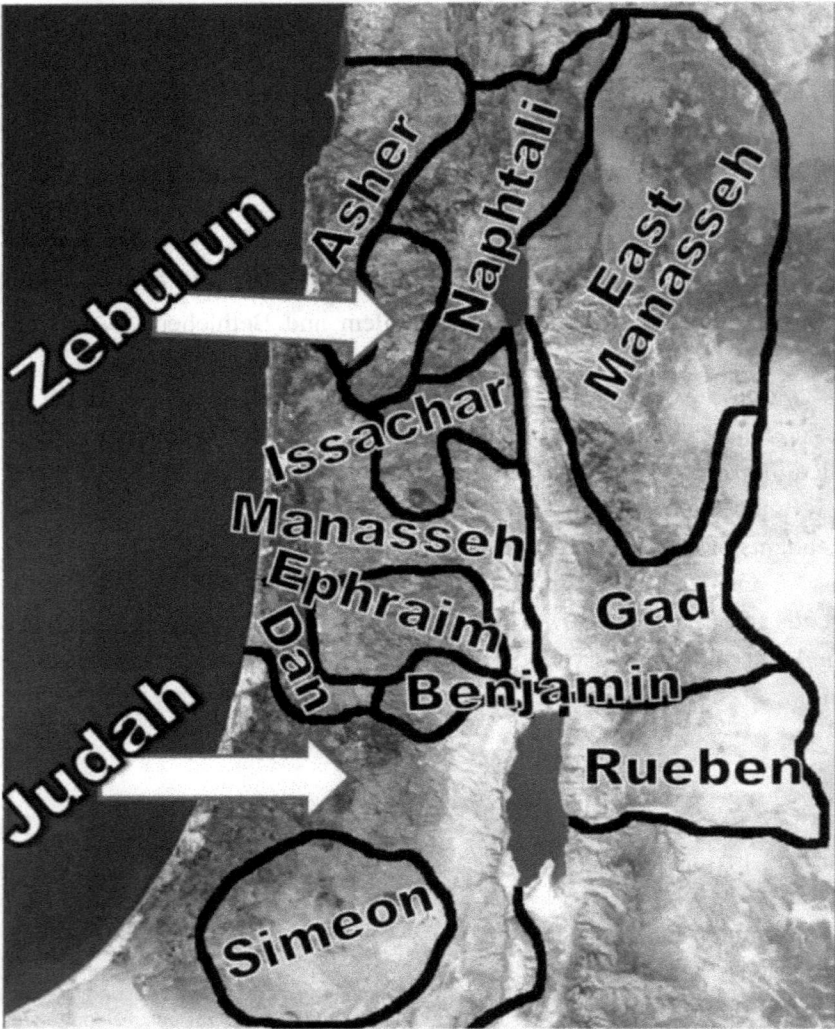

Figure 6 - 4

By the time of Jesus' birth, Bethlehem would have contained a concentration of descendants from the tribes of Judah and Benjamin who resettled that area after returning from the Babylonian deportation. Thus, a number of the children within Bethlehem would have descended from Rachel, mother of Benjamin. Jeremiah's prophecy portrays the figure of Rachel crying out from her grave near Ramah, lamenting the death of the young boys of Bethlehem, many of which would have descended as "her children."[523]

Review of Matthew's Text (Matthew 2:13-18)

13 After they departed, listen up, an angel of the Lord appeared to Joseph in a dream, saying, "Arise, take the Child and His mother and flee into Egypt. Stay there until I tell you, because Herod is about to search for the Child to destroy Him."

14 Then, after getting up, he took the Child and His mother and departed by night into Egypt. 15 Now, he stayed there until Herod's death, that the thing spoken by the Lord through Hosea might be fulfilled, saying, "Out of Egypt I called My Son."

16 Then Herod, seeing that he had been made a fool of by the Magi, became very angry. Consequently, based on the exact time he had learned from the Magi, he sent out an order to kill all the boys from two years and under in Bethlehem and the surrounding area.

17 Then the word spoken through the prophet Jeremiah was fulfilled, saying, 18 "A sound of much crying and lamenting was heard in Ramah — Rachel, crying over her children, and she did not want to be comforted because they are no more." (BT)

---

[523] Matthew 2:18 BT

CHAPTER 7

....

Going Home

Herod's bloody reign ended the spring of 4 B.C. as he gasped his last breath in the city of Jericho. Imagine Joseph's relief upon hearing the news. Picture the delight on Mary's face as Joseph told her they could go home.

Matthew's Text (Matthew 2:19-23)[524]

19 Now, when Herod died, listen, an angel of the Lord appeared to Joseph in a dream in Egypt 20 saying, "Arise, take the Child and His mother and travel to the land of Israel. For those seeking the life of the Child have died." 21 Therefore, he arose and took the Child and His mother and went into the land of Israel.

22 Now, having heard that Archelaus was ruler of Judea instead of his father Herod, Joseph was afraid to go there. Thus having been warned in a dream, he departed to the region of Galilee. 23 Then, after arriving, he resided in the town called Nazareth, so that the word spoken through the prophets might be fulfilled — that Jesus would be called a Nazarene.[525] (BT)

---

[524] No passages within the books of Mark, Luke, or John parallel Matthew 2:19-23.

[525] Nazarene – a person from the town of Nazareth

Those Seeking the Child Have Died (Matthew 2:19)

Multiple Conspirators

"Those seeking the life of the Child have died,"[526] the angel announced to Joseph. His use of the word "those" points to multiple personalities. *Hoi* (hŏĭ),[527] the Greek word translated "those," forms a plural *masculine* article. Since the angel employed a plural masculine article, the plot against Jesus involved more than one male. Antipater,[528] Herod the Great's son, almost certainly collaborated with his father in the plan to murder the young boys of Bethlehem.[529]

Antipater

Antipater's ruthless hunger for power matched that of his father. He desperately desired to succeed Herod as king and manipulated family rivalries to position himself as the heir apparent. For example, he deceived King Herod into believing Alexander and Aristobulus, Antipater's older brothers, conspired against the throne. As a result, Herod put them both to death in 7 B.C.

The Magi's quest to find "the One who has been born King of the Jews"[530] would have disturbed Antipater as much as it troubled Herod. Considering Antipater's motives for persuading his father to eliminate Alexander and Aristobulus, Antipater could have joined forces with Herod to pursue Jesus' life as well.

---

[526] Matthew 2:19 BT

[527] *Hoi* (hŏĭ), οἱ

[528] Antipater (ăn-tĭ-pə-tər)

[529] Take care to differentiate between Herod's son, Antipater, and Herod's father, also named Antipater.

[530] Matthew 2:2 BT

Herod's Restraint of Antipater

The continuous evil acts of Antipater seemed excessive even to Herod the Great. Consequently, Herod threw him into prison. Herod then sent word to Caesar Augustus requesting permission to address Antipater's outrageously wicked conduct. (Josephus, 1977, p. 364)[531] Not long before Herod's own death, Caesar granted him the option to imprison Antipater indefinitely or to execute him. (Josephus, 1977, p. 366)[532]

Meanwhile, Antipater attempted to bribe his jailer with promises to do "great things" for him if only he would open the cell door.[533] The jailer loyally informed Herod of Antipater's proposal. Upon hearing the report, Herod ordered Antipater's execution without further delay. (Josephus, 1977, p. 366)[534]

Five days later, Herod died in the city of Jericho. (Josephus, 1977, p. 366)[535] When the angel informed Joseph, "those seeking the life of the Child have died," neither Herod nor Antipater remained a threat.[536]

---

[531] *The Antiquities of the Jews*, Book 17, Chapter 5, Paragraph 8; Titus Flavius Josephus (jō-sĕ́-fəs), a Jewish general and historian, lived 37-100 A.D. For more information regarding Josephus, see "Appendix 3: Glossary."

[532] *The Antiquities of the Jews*, Book 17, Chapter 7, Paragraph 1

[533] *The Antiquities of the Jews*, Book 17, Chapter 7, Paragraph 1

[534] *The Antiquities of the Jews*, Book 17, Chapter 8, Paragraph 1

[535] *The Antiquities of the Jews*, Book 17, Chapter 8, Paragraphs 1-2

[536] Matthew 2:20 BT

***

Contemplation Points

1. Have you ever moved "back home" after living away for an extended period?
   a. If so, how did you feel when you found out you were moving back home?
   b. What emotions did you experience when you arrived back home?
   c. What challenges did you face upon your return? How did you cope?
2. Consider Joseph and Mary's move back to Nazareth, their hometown.
   a. How might they have felt when the angel announced they could go home?
   b. What emotions might they have experienced when they arrived home?
   c. What challenges might they have faced upon their return? How might they have coped?

Archelaus Was Ruler (Matthew 2:22)

Following Herod's death, Caesar Augustus assigned Archelaus the regions of Samaria, Judea, and Idumea (about half of Herod the Great's kingdom) and gave him the title Ethnarch[537] of the Tetrarchy[538] of Judea.

Map: Territory Inherited by Herod's Sons

| Philip – Tetrarchy of Betanea |
| Antipas – Tetrarchy of Galilee |
| Archelaus – Tetrarchy of Judea |

Figure 7 - 1

---

[537] Ethnarch – "Ruler of a Nation"
[538] Tetrarchy – one fourth of a Roman client kingdom or province

Afraid to Go There (Matthew 2:22)

Returning to his homeland, Joseph intended to settle in the southern region of Judea, most likely in Bethlehem. However, Archelaus controlled the area, and his brutal corruption exceeded his father's wickedness. Alarmed at the prospect of living under Archelaus' rule, Joseph altered his plan.

The manner in which Archelaus addressed civil discontent exemplifies his ruthlessness. Two Jewish teachers, Judas and Matthias, led their students to tear down the golden Roman eagle Herod the Great had mounted over the Temple gate. (Josephus, 1977, pp. 364-365)[539] On March 12, 4 B.C., shortly before his death, Herod ordered his soldiers to burn alive the two educators and 40 or so of their pupils. About a month later, a day before the Passover celebration, numerous Jews openly protested the fate of Judas and Matthias. By that time, Herod had died and Archelaus controlled the region of Judea. Upon receiving reports of the public demonstration, into the midst of the festivities Archelaus deployed soldiers who then massacred around 3,000 celebrants. (Josephus, 1977, pp. 367-368)[540]

Through a dream, God warned Joseph of the hazardous political environment in Judea. Therefore, Joseph continued northward to his hometown in Galilee, hoping to ensure the welfare of his family. For Antipas, who ruled Galilee, proved less menacing than his brother, Archelaus.

---

[539] *The Antiquities of the Jews*, Book 17, Chapter 6, Paragraphs 2-4
[540] *The Antiquities of the Jews*, Book 17, Chapter 9, Paragraphs 1-3

Galilee (Matthew 2:22)

Galilee, situated north of Judea, consisted of the most densely populated region ruled under the Herodian dynasty.

Map: Region of Galilee

Figure 7 - 2

In 734 B.C., more than 700 years before Jesus' birth, King Tiglath-pileser of Assyria conquered the region that later became Roman Galilee.[541] He deported a large part of the Israelite population to distant Assyrian lands[542] and repopulated the region with Aramaic-speaking Gentile[543]

---

[541] For more information about Tiglath-pileser's conquest of the Kingdom of Israel, see "Chapter 2 – Kings & Scoundrels: Jesus' Ancestors," heading "The Babylonian Deportation (Matthew 1:11)," subheading "Assyrian Deportation (of Israel)."

[542] 2 Kings 15:27-29

[543] The Jews identified anyone not of Jacob's bloodline as a Gentile. God gave Jacob, son of Isaac and grandson of Abraham, the name Israel (Genesis 32:28).

captives from other nations he had conquered. Over centuries of interaction with the displaced Gentiles, a distinct Aramaic dialect spoken with a coarse accent developed among the remaining Galilean Jews.[544] The Jews of the southern region of Judea looked down on the Galileans of the north, considering themselves more culturally pure.

Eleven of Jesus' original twelve apostles came from Galilee.[545] Judas Iscariot, who betrayed Jesus, did not. *Iscariot*, a transliteration[546] of an Aramaic word, means "man of Kerioth," a village in the southern region of Judea about 30 miles[547] south of Jerusalem.

Galilee: Jordan River Valley North of the Sea of Galilee (About 1920 A.D.)

Figure 7 - 3

---

[544] Matthew 26:73

[545] Mark 14:70; Acts 1:11; 2:7

[546] When transliterating, instead of translating a word, a translator *spells out* an approximation of the original language's *pronunciation* of the word using the alphabet of the second language. For more details regarding transliteration, see "Appendix 3: Glossary."

[547] 48 kilometers

He Resided in Nazareth (Matthew 2:23)

Upon returning to Nazareth of Galilee, his hometown, Joseph continued the trade of craftsman[548] and raised a family with Mary. Matthew, Mark, Luke, and John all mentioned Nazareth in their writings. However, no Old Testament book refers to the town, nor does Josephus or the Talmud.[549] Nazareth merited no special attention until the day God's angel Gabriel delivered a divine message to Mary.[550]

Nazareth lay about 66 miles[551] north of Bethlehem, nestled upon the northwestern slope of Nazareth Valley. The valley's spring could have provided water for a village of around 2,000 inhabitants. Supplemented by cisterns, in common use at that time, the population might have grown larger. Nazareth's size supported a synagogue.[552]

A six-hour, 14-mile[553] walk northeast of Nazareth led to the Sea of Galilee. A trip southward to Bethlehem required a journey of about a week. Sepphoris,[554] a city visible from Nazareth on a neighboring hilltop, lay about three miles[555] northwest, an hour walk through the valley between the two.

Antipas ruled the Tetrarchy of Galilee after the death of his father, Herod the Great, and selected Sepphoris as his capital.[556] Following his launch of a massive construction project to build up the city, it quickly grew

---

[548] For more information concerning Joseph's trade, see "Chapter 3 – Birth of Jesus, Rescuer of His People," heading "Joseph (1:18)," subheading "Joseph the Craftsman."

[549] The Talmud contains traditional teachings of ancient Jewish religious scholars, not God-inspired Scripture.

[550] Luke 1:26

[551] 106 kilometers

[552] Not until sometime after 200 A.D. did Jewish tradition dictate that a location inhabited by ten or more Israelite men must have a synagogue. As Merrill Unger explains, "In the post-Talmudic period it was required that a synagogue should be built wherever ten Israelites were dwelling together." (Unger, 1988, heading "Synagogue," subheading "Where Located")

[553] 23 kilometers

[554] Sepphoris (sĕf-ŏ-rĭs)

[555] Five kilometers

[556] In 18 A.D., Antipas established the city of Tiberias on the western shore of the Sea of Galilee and moved his center of government there from Sepphoris. Nonetheless, his vast reconstruction of Sepphoris continued.

to a population of 15,000 – 20,000. Antipas' long-term development of Sepphoris lasted throughout Jesus' lifetime, providing ample employment opportunities for craftsmen[557] of the area like Joseph and his sons.

Map: Nazareth & Bethlehem

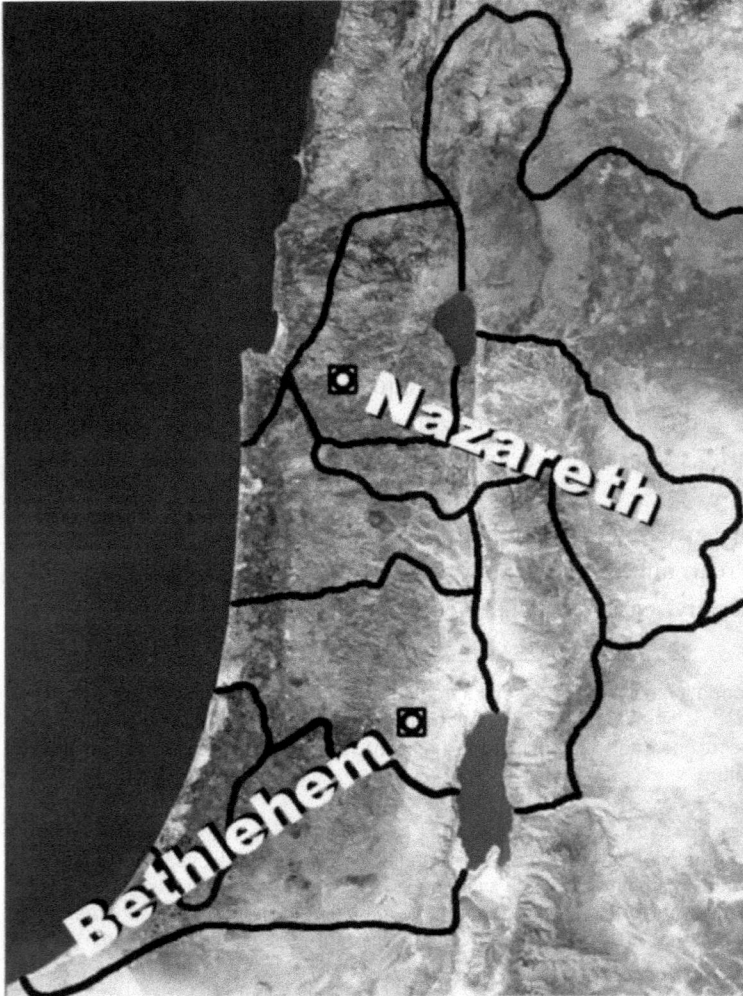

Figure 7 - 4

---

[557] For more information concerning Joseph's trade, see "Chapter 3 – Birth of Jesus, Rescuer of His People," heading "Joseph (1:18)," subheading "Joseph the Craftsman."

Nazareth (About 1860 A.D.)

Figure 7 - 5

Nazareth (1932 A.D.)

Figure 7 - 6

Nazareth (About 1898 A.D.)

Figure 7 - 7

Nazareth (About 1940 A.D.)

Figure 7 - 8

Jesus Would Be Called a Nazarene (Matthew 2:23)

Scriptural Error?

Matthew explained that Jesus grew up in Nazareth "so that the word spoken through the prophets might be fulfilled: that Jesus would be called a Nazarene."[558] Nevertheless, not one Old Testament book contains such a prophecy. Consequently, Matthew's statement ignites the curiosity of prudent Bible students. Does Matthew's assertion generate a conflict within the Scriptures? If not, how is it that Matthew alleged "the prophets" foretold Jesus would be a Nazarene? A rational investigation shows Matthew did not err.

Not All Prophecy Was Written

God did not require His prophets to compile an exhaustive written account of their prophecies. Neither Abraham nor Elijah wrote Scripture, yet both remained renowned prophets.[559] The list below contains a sampling of the names of lesser-known prophets who did not write down their teachings.

- Abel[560]
- Ahijah[561]
- Enoch[562]
- Jehu[563]
- Oded[564]

Furthermore, Matthew spoke of a plurality of prophets whom God made aware the Messiah would come from Nazareth. He did not intend to refer his readers to a specific passage of Scripture written by any particular prophet. Otherwise, as elsewhere in his book,[565] he would have

---

[558] Matthew 2:23 BT

[559] Genesis 20:1-7 (Note verse 7.); 1 Kings 18:36

[560] Luke 11:49-51 (Note verse 51.)

[561] 1 Kings 11:29

[562] Jude 14

[563] 1 Kings 16:1-13 (Note verses 1, 7, and 12.); Take care not to confuse Jehu the prophet with Jehu, King of Israel.

[564] 2 Chronicles 15:8

[565] Matthew 1:22-23; 2:15; 2:17-18; 3:3; 4:4-16; 8:17; 12:17-21; 13:35; 21:4-5; 27:9-10

- Referred to "the prophet" (singular) instead of "the *prophets*" (plural),
- Given the name of the prophet, or
- Provided a quote from the prophet's writings.

Oral Prophecy

The list above provides examples of the many prophets who did not write Scripture. The fact that God did not have them document their teaching does not imply He did not use them to deliver divine communications. They delivered God's messages *orally*, not in script. As a result, we know little of those devout men other than what biblical authors wrote about them.

Most Christians recognize the names of prophets who wrote Scripture, among them Old Testament personalities such as Moses, Joshua, Samuel, Ezra, Nehemiah, David, Solomon, Isaiah, Jeremiah, Ezekiel, and Daniel. Most would also know the names of Matthew, Mark, Luke, John, Paul, James, Peter, and Jude – prophets who wrote the histories and correspondence of the New Testament.

Those better-known prophets put in writing much of what they taught. At times, they referred to the unwritten oral prophecies of earlier prophets. For example, Jude quoted an unwritten oral prophecy of Enoch.[566] Similarly, Matthew confirmed that prophets of old declared the Messiah would arise out of Nazareth.[567]

Inspiration

The teachings that foretold Jesus would emerge from Nazareth rest among the many prophetic statements never logged in the books of the Old Testament. How did Matthew become aware of those prophecies? He penned *God's own* account of the life of Jesus. He did not write autonomously, for "all Scripture is inspired by God."[568]

---

[566] Jude 14
[567] Matthew 2:23
[568] 2 Timothy 3:16 NASU

Speaking of God's attributes, David wrote, "You know it all."[569] God knew the unwritten prophecies that identified the Messiah as a Nazarene, because the messages of all the prophets originated in the mind of God.[570] God imparted His knowledge to Matthew. Consequently, Matthew's statement that "the prophets" foretold "that Jesus would be called a Nazarene" stands firm.

Review of Matthew's Text (Matthew 2:19-23)

19 Now, when Herod died, listen, an angel of the Lord appeared to Joseph in a dream in Egypt 20 saying, "Arise, and take the Child and His mother, and travel to the land of Israel. For those seeking the life of the Child have died." 21 Therefore, he arose and took the Child and His mother, and went into the land of Israel.

22 Now, having heard that Archelaus was ruler of Judea instead of his father, Herod, Joseph was afraid to go there. Thus having been warned in a dream, he departed to the region of Galilee. 23 Then, after arriving, he resided in the town called Nazareth, so that the word spoken through the prophets might be fulfilled — that Jesus would be called a Nazarene.[571] (BT)

---

[569] Psalm 139:4 NASU

[570] Christians must understand that God spoke through Matthew (2 Timothy 3:16-17; 2 Peter 1:20-21). The thoughts God delivered through Matthew reflect Matthew's own style and vocabulary in the same way a writer's communication exhibits the style and color of his chosen pen and ink.

[571] Nazarene – a person from the town of Nazareth

CHAPTER 8

....

The Desert Prophet

Soon after the angel notified Mary she would conceive a Son through the Holy Spirit, she journeyed far southward from Nazareth to the hill country of Judea to visit her relative, Elizabeth. By the time Mary arrived, Elizabeth's pregnancy had progressed about six months.[572] Three months later, Elizabeth gave birth to a son and named him John. John the Immerser,[573] as the public would come to refer to him, grew up to serve as a prophet of God.

Matthew's Text (Matthew 3:1-6)[574]

1 Now, in those days, John the Immerser came proclaiming in the Judean Desert, saying, 2 "Repent, for the Kingdom of the Heavens has come near." 3 For this was he who was spoken of through the prophet Isaiah, saying, "A voice crying aloud in the desert, 'Prepare the Lord's way. Make His paths straight.'"

---

[572] Luke 1:35-40

[573] Immerser – *Baptistés* (Bӓp-tǐs-tӑs, βαπτιστής), the Greek word translated "Immerser," often finds itself *transliterated* as "Baptist," instead of *translated* precisely as "Immerser." For more information about John, see "Chapter 8 – The Desert Prophet." For a discussion of the origin of the word "Baptist," see "Chapter 8 – The Desert Prophet," heading "They Were Immersed (Matthew 3:6)."

[574] Mark 1:2-6 and Luke 3:3-6 parallel Matthew 3:1-6. John contains no parallel passage.

> *₄ Now, John, himself, wore camel hair clothing, together with a skin belt around his waist. And his food was locusts and wild honey. ₅ Jerusalem and all Judea, as well as the entire region around the Jordan, came out to him. ₆ And, they were immersed in the Jordan River by him, acknowledging their sins.* (BT)

John the Immerser (Matthew 3:1)

John's Youth

John the Immerser grew up a city[575] boy within the hill country of Judea, in a godly household. His father Zacharias served as a priest.[576] His mother Elizabeth descended from the priestly line of Aaron as well.[577] Luke wrote, "They were both righteous in the sight of God, walking blamelessly in all the commandments and requirements of the Lord."[578]

The Boys

John was about six months older than Jesus. Since their mothers shared an exceptional bond, the boys probably interacted from time to time. As children, they likely met up each year[579] at the Passover festival, as well as at the annual Pentecost festival and Feast of Booths.[580] Imagine their playful conversations as they explored the Temple grounds together.

---

[575] For information regarding the city in which John grew up, see "Chapter 3 – Birth of Jesus, Rescuer of His People," heading "Mary (Matthew 1:18)," subheading "Daring Character."

[576] Luke 1:5

[577] Luke 1:5

[578] Luke 1:5-6 NASU

[579] Jesus would have attended the Passover celebration each year as He grew up, for Luke says Joseph and Mary "went to Jerusalem every year at the Feast of the Passover" (Luke 2:41-42 NASU).

[580] Deuteronomy 16:16; Exodus 23:14-17; 34:18-24

Judean Desert (Matthew 3:1)

John the Immerser moved from his native hill country to the Judean Desert (also known as the Wilderness of Judah). The Scriptures do not discuss his motive for relocating, nor do they tell the number of years he had resided there by the time Jesus visited. However, Matthew and Mark indicate John had lived in the desert long enough to have adopted the customs of the local people, including their dress and diet.[581]

The Judean Desert, a desolate tract of land east of Jerusalem within the huge Jordan valley, extends westward from the Dead Sea shore and northward along both sides of the Jordan River. In spite of its mountainous terrain and scarcity of trees, this wilderness hosted a few villages populated by resilient individuals.

Judean Desert: North Shore of Dead Sea in Background (About 1898 A.D.)

Figure 8 - 1

---

[581] Matthew 3:4; Mark 1:6

Judean Desert (About 1900 A.D.)

Figure 8 - 2

Judean Desert (About 1934 A.D.)

Figure 8 - 3

Bethany Beyond the Jordan

John the Immerser based his operations at least part of the time in a community called *Bethany beyond the Jordan*.[582] Although the site remains uninhabited today, archaeologists have excavated the ruins of Bethany. Artifacts found there date from the early Roman era through the sixth century A.D.

The remnants of the village lie adjacent to Ain Kharrar, the spring that feeds a stream called Wadi el-Kharrar. The creek flows westward about one mile[583] from the site of the village before draining into the Jordan River. Marshy wetland covers much of the terrain between Bethany and the river. Thickets become increasingly dense as one draws closer to the Jordan.

Map: Bethany Beyond the Jordan

Figure 8 - 4

---

[582] John 1:28 NASU
[583] 1.5 kilometers

Jordan River Bank near Bethany (About 1910 A.D.)

Figure 8 - 5

Repent (Matthew 3:2)

John the Immerser delivered his divine message to anyone who would listen, proclaiming everyone should, "Repent, for the Kingdom of the Heavens has come near."[584] The Greek word translated "repent," *metanoeíte* (mĕ-tä-nŏ-ĕí-tĕ),[585] appears as a conjugated[586] form of the infinitive[587] *metanoéo* (mĕt-ä-nŏ-ĕ́-ō).[588] *Metanoéo* combines two Greek words; *metá*,[589] which denotes "after," and *noéo*,[590] meaning "to think carefully." It signifies the changing of one's thoughts and behavior as the result of deliberate consideration. John warned those practicing sin to change their lifestyle because "the Kingdom of the Heavens has come near."[591]

---

[584] Matthew 3:2 BT

[585] *Metanoeíte* (mĕ-tä-nŏ-ĕí-tĕ), μετανοεῖτε

[586] Conjugated – A conjugated form of an infinitive reflects the number, person, tense, etc. that a writer intends to communicate.

[587] Infinitive – a verb form with no indication of person, number, mood, or tense (Examples of infinitives include *to eat, to run,* and *to swim*.)

[588] *Metanoeo* (mĕ-tä-nŏ-ĕ́-ō), μετανοέω

[589] *Metá* (mĕ-tá), μετά

[590] *Noĕo* (nŏ-ĕ́-ō), νοέω

[591] Matthew 3:2 BT

The Kingdom of the Heavens (Matthew 3:2)

Three Heavens

Three heavens existed within the Jewish mindset of the first century A.D. They considered the first heaven to be the *sky* above the earth, where clouds, storms, thunder, and lightning form. They viewed the second heaven as *outer space*, where the sun, moon, and stars reside. In their third heaven, the *Kingdom of Heaven*, lives God, and righteous spirits hold citizenship.

Jesus' apostle Paul wrote that God transported him to the third heaven for a short time. Paul referred to it as "Paradise." Although God exposed Paul to the spiritual realm, He forbade him to share the details of what he had heard during his brief visit.[592]

Kingdom Synonyms

Matthew frequently cited Jesus as having used the expressions "Kingdom," "Kingdom of the Heavens,"[593] and "Kingdom of God." Likewise, he attributed the use of the phrase "Kingdom of the Heavens" to John the Immerser,[594] as well as to the apostles when they spoke as a group.[595] Curiously though, Matthew chose simply to use the word "Kingdom" when speaking for himself and not quoting the words of someone else.[596]

When on trial before the Roman governor Pilate, Jesus spoke of the Kingdom as "My Kingdom."[597] When He told Peter, "I will build My church," Jesus synonymously referred to His church as "the Kingdom of

---

[592] 2 Corinthians 12:1-4

[593] New Testament writers utilized both "heaven" and "heavens" synonymously to communicate exactly the same thing, making no distinction in meaning between the singular and plural forms of the word. In order to remain as closely parallel to Matthew's original words as practical, the Bagby Translation (BT) employs the plural *heavens* each time Matthew utilized the plural form of the word in his Greek text.

[594] Matthew 3:2 BT

[595] Matthew 18:1 BT

[596] Matthew 4:23; 9:35 BT

[597] John 18:36 NASU

the Heavens" in the next sentence.[598] Paul identified the Kingdom as "the Kingdom of Christ and God."[599]

All the synonymous expressions discussed above describe the group of individuals who have pledged their ultimate loyalty to Jesus, who called them "My Kingdom" and "My church." He classified them as "the Kingdom of the *Heavens*," as opposed to any kingdom consisting of earthly terrain and political intrigue.

United Kingdom

Jesus united godly people "to be a kingdom."[600] Because they chose to live their lives "in a manner worthy of God," He invited them to be citizens of His Kingdom.[601] Jesus "transferred" their citizenship from the "domain of darkness" into His own kingdom.[602] Hence, when John the Immerser advised his listeners, "the Kingdom of the Heavens has come near," he spoke of Jesus' imminent establishment of His church, to whom He would grant citizenship in the Kingdom of the Heavens.

Make His Paths Straight (Matthew 3:3)

When royalty of ancient Eastern nations traveled cross-country, forerunners customarily ventured far ahead along the intended course. They prepared the way for the passage of the monarch by doing anything necessary to make the journey safe, comfortable, and uneventful. Those forward scouts plugged holes and removed rocks from the roadway. If needed, they constructed new sections of straight road where they deemed the existing route too crooked. On occasion, they filled deep valleys and leveled steep hills.[603]

John the Immerser served as Jesus' forerunner, tasked to "prepare the Lord's way" and "make His paths straight."[604] He readied the twisted,

---

[598] Matthew 16:18-19 BT
[599] Ephesians 5:5 NASU
[600] Revelation 1:4-6 NASU
[601] 1 Thessalonians 2:12 NASU
[602] Colossians 1:13-14 NASU
[603] Isaiah 40:3-5
[604] Matthew 3:3 BT

stony hearts of the Jewish population for the arrival of the Messiah.

Camel Hair Clothing with a Skin Belt (Matthew 3:4)

Camel Hair Clothing

Like the country folk surrounding him in the Judean Desert, John dressed in camel hair clothing. City-dwelling scribes[605] and Pharisees[606] drew attention by adorning themselves with extravagantly designed attire.[607] In contrast, John did not don regal apparel, in spite of his noble purpose in life.[608] His style of dress reflected his wilderness environment.

As a camel shed its hair toward the end of spring, weavers collected long, shaggy strands from its back, hump, and neck. They then threaded the hair into an economical, bristly material. Camel drivers and shepherds in Eastern countries wore camel hair garments as late as the early 21st century.

Camel's Hair (1939 A.D.)

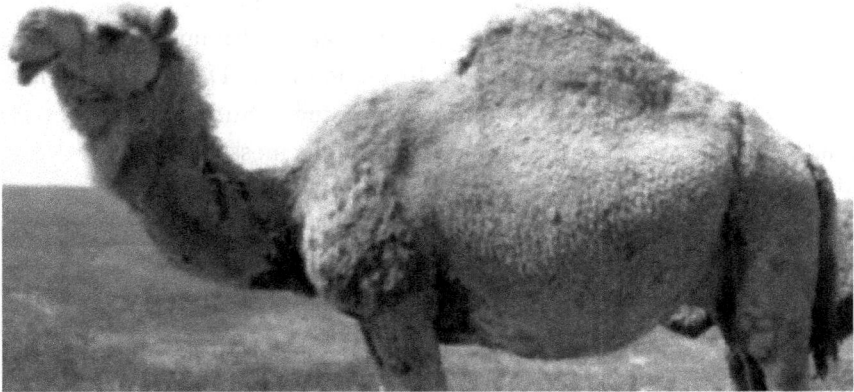

Figure 8 - 6

---

[605] For more information concerning the scribes, see "Chapter 4 – The Magi Meet Herod, King of Judea," heading "Who Were the Scribes? (Matthew 2:4)."

[606] For more information concerning the Pharisee sect, see "Chapter 9 – Poisonous Snakes: Pharisees & Sadducees," heading "Who Were the Pharisees? (Matthew 3:7)."

[607] Matthew 23:2,5

[608] Matthew 11:7-9; Luke 7:24-26

Camels Grazing near Nazareth (About 1894 A.D.)

Figure 8 - 7

Skin Belt

Scribes, Pharisees, and Sadducees[609] who ventured outside Jerusalem to hear John's proclamations dressed impressively, wrapping a stunning sash around their waist. In contrast, John the Immerser girded himself country style, with a long strip of animal skin trimmed to size, the fitting accessory to a camel hair wardrobe in the Judean Desert. He did not attempt to impress his listeners with lavish costume. Sufficient command and influence flowed from the divine source of his message.

Locusts and Wild Honey (Matthew 3:4)

Locusts

John the Immerser maintained eating habits as rural as the manner in which he dressed. He ate as other inhabitants of the wilderness, dining on a variety of foods including locust and honey.

Similar in appearance to grasshoppers, locusts hop, fly, and often gather in a swarm. God's dietary instructions within the Old Covenant Law of Moses permitted the Israelites to eat locusts.[610]

---

[609] For more information concerning the Sadducee sect, see "Chapter 9 – Poisonous Snakes: Pharisees & Sadducees," heading "Who Were the Sadducees? (Matthew 3:7)."
[610] Leviticus 11:22

Pink Locust of Israel

Figure 8 - 8

Pink Locust Swarm (During Plague of 1915 A.D.)

Figure 8 - 9

A person preparing locusts for consumption first removes the entrails. After grilling, he discards the legs and head before serving the remaining portion. Albert Barnes described his observation of the cooking of locusts in Middle-Eastern countries during the mid-1850s. He wrote,

> *They stick them in long rows upon wooden spits, roast them at the fire, and then proceed to devour them with great zest. There are also other ways of preparing them. For example: they cook them and dress them in oil; or, having dried them, they pulverize them, and, when other food is scarce, make bread of the meal. ... When the Arabs have them in quantities they roast or dry them in an oven, or boil them and eat them with salt. The Arabs in the kingdom of Morocco boil the locusts; and the Bedouins eat locusts, which are collected in great quantities in the beginning of April, when they are easily caught. After having been roasted a little upon the iron plate on which bread is baked, they are dried in the sun, and then put into large sacks, with the mixture of a little salt.* (Barnes, 1997, heading "Matthew 3:4," subheading "His Meat Was Locusts")

Wild Honey

John the Immerser also ate wild honey. Bees produce honey within the crevices of rocks in Israel, not just in trees.[611] Easily accessible, honey became a staple of the rural diet.

---

[611] Deuteronomy 32:13; Psalm 81:16

They Were Immersed (Matthew 3:6)

Individuals seeking to please God traveled to John from distant places, including "Jerusalem and all Judea, as well as the entire region around the Jordan, ... And they were immersed in the Jordan River by him."[612]

Greek

The Greek word e*baptídzonto* (ĕ-băp-tǐ-dzŏn-tŏ),[613] traditionally rendered "were baptized," literally means "were immersed." Why, then, do so many translations insert "were baptized" instead of "were immersed" in Matthew 3:6? The history of the word "baptize" reveals the reason.

Latin

Tertullian

The term "baptize" came to English through Latin. Tertullian,[614] the first writer to produce an extensive body of Christian literature in Latin, completed *De Baptismo* (Concerning Baptism) around 200 A.D., a book in which he chose to transliterate[615] the Greek word *báptisma*[616] into Latin as *baptismo*, instead of properly translating it as *immersio* (Latin for "immersion"). He likely utilized this transliteration instead of a precise translation to avoid a clash with peers, many of whom taught pouring a little water over a person's head could replace immersion. Even so, he described an immersion process when he wrote,

---

[612] Matthew 3:5-6 BT

[613] *Ebaptídzonto* (ĕ-băp-tǐ-dzŏn-tŏ), ἐβαπτίζοντο; third person plural imperfect passive of the Greek infinitive *baptídzo* (băp-tǐ-dzō), βαπτίζω, which means "to immerse"

[614] Tertullian lived from about 160 A.D. to 225 A.D. in the city of Carthage, within the Roman province of Africa.

[615] When transliterating, instead of translating a word, a translator *spells out* an approximation of the original language's *pronunciation* of the word, using the alphabet of the second language. For more details regarding transliteration, see "Appendix 3: Glossary."

[616] *Báptisma* (băp-tǐs-mä), βάπτισμα

> *A man is lowered into water and with intervals for a few words is dipped, and rises up again not much cleaner or even no cleaner, and yet an incredible result in eternity is deemed to be assured.*[617]
> (Tertullian, 1919, p. 47)

Tertullian's academic compromise in the form of using indistinct vocabulary (*baptismo* instead of *immersio*), predisposed Christianity to misunderstanding for centuries without end.

Jerome

Jerome,[618] in his 405 A.D. Latin translation of the Scriptures, followed Tertullian's example when he transliterated the Greek *ebaptídzonto* ("were immersed") into Latin as *baptizabantur,*[619] instead of translating it precisely. Latin speakers of Jerome's day used any of three synonyms to convey the meaning of the Greek *ebaptídzonto* ("were immersed"); *mersabantur,*[620] *mergebantur,*[621] and *demergebantur.*[622] Most likely, Jerome avoided these direct translations to avert conflict with his superiors, who taught pouring a little water over a person's head could replace immersion.[623] As a result, the Roman Catholic Church institutionalized the transliterations *baptize* and *baptism* in lieu of the precise translations, "immerse" and "immersion."

---

[617] *De Baptismo* (Concerning Baptism) by Tertullian, Chapter 2

[618] Jerome – a Roman Catholic priest

[619] *Baptizabantur* (bäp-tē-zä-bän-tür)

[620] *Mersabantur* (mĕr-sä-bán-tür); third person plural imperfect passive of the Latin infinitive *mersare* (mĕr-sä-rĕ), to immerse

[621] *Mergebantur* (mĕr-gä-bán-tür); third person plural imperfect passive of the Latin infinitive *mergere* (mĕr-gĕ-rĕ), to immerse, to plunge

[622] *Demergebantur* (dā-mĕr-gä-bán-tür); third person plural imperfect passive of the Latin infinitive *demargere* (dā-mĕr-gĕ-rĕ), to immerse, to submerge

[623] If John had poured water over the penitent, Matthew would have employed the Greek verb *epikéo* (ĕ-pĭ-kĕ́-ō), ἐπιχέω, which means "to pour upon." If John had sprinkled water on the penitent, Matthew would have used the Greek verb *rhantídzo* (rhän-tĭ́-dzo), ῥαντίζω, which means "to sprinkle." Instead, Matthew and all other New Testament writers consistently utilized the Greek verb *baptídzo* (bäp-tĭ́-dzō), βαπτίζω, which means "to immerse."

Thus began Ecclesiastical Latin,[624] the mother of *church speak*.[625] *Church speak*, ambiguous vocabulary typically confined to *traditional* Christian religious discussion, tends to blur the definition of words employed by biblical authors and often leads Bible readers to misunderstand God's Scriptures. Distorting the meaning intended by God's prophets, Jerome and his colleagues invented the obscure Latin infinitive *baptizare*,[626] "to baptize," defining the new word to correspond to their doctrinal tradition.

English

Ecclesiastical pressures to conform to Jerome's Latin Vulgate[627] translation weighed heavily on scholars who later translated the Scriptures into other languages. Consistent with Jerome's deviation from the prophets' Greek texts, the transliterations "baptize," "baptism," and John the "Baptist" replaced the precise translations "immerse," "immersion," and John the "Immerser." Jerome could have prevented centuries of misunderstanding and debate had he *translated* these words from the Greek instead of *transliterating* them into Latin.

---

[624] Ecclesiastical Latin, utilized by the Roman Catholic Church when publishing official documents, contains distinctive Latin vocabulary devised by Roman Catholic leaders over the centuries, as opposed to secular Latin vocabulary.

[625] For more information about church speak, see the heading "Church Speak" within "Appendix 2: The Bagby Translation."

[626] *Baptizare* (băp-tē-zá-rĕ)

[627] Historians and linguists typically refer to Jerome's translation as the Latin Vulgate.

Jordan River (Matthew 3:6)

Source of the Jordan River

John typically remained near the Jordan River because he required "much water"[628] in which to immerse penitent believers. The Jordan River begins with the union of three streams: the Dan, Banias, and Hasbani. The *Dan*,[629] principal source of the Jordan, flows from Dan Spring where the city of Dan once stood. The *Banias*[630] originates at Banias Spring near the ruins of the ancient city of Caesarea Philippi and merges with the Dan about five miles[631] south of Dan Spring. The *Hasbani*,[632] with the Wazzani River as its primary tributary, joins the Dan about a mile[633] downstream from the confluence of the Banias and Dan rivers.

Dan River (About 1898 A.D.)

Figure 8 - 10

---

[628] John 3:23 NASU
[629] Dan River, also called Leddan River
[630] Banias River, also called Hermon River
[631] Eight kilometers
[632] Hasbani River, also called Snir River
[633] 1.6 kilometers

Banias River (About 1898 A.D.)

Figure 8 - 11

Hasbani River (About 1900 A.D.)

Figure 8 - 12

Route of the Jordan River

In ancient times, the Jordan River flowed 11 miles[634] before spilling into the northern shore of a small lake named Huleh.[635] Israeli officials drained the marshlands of the Huleh Valley in the 1950s A.D., and only a section of the lake remains. The basin became Israel's first national nature reserve and the Jordan River continues to run through it.

Huleh Valley (About 1940 A.D.)

Figure 8 - 13

Lake Huleh (About 1920 A.D.)

Figure 8 - 14

---

[634] 18 kilometers
[635] Huleh (hŭ-lə) Lake, sometimes spelled Hula, also called "Merom" in Joshua 11:5,7

During the time of John the Immerser, the Jordan River continued four miles[636] through Lake Huleh and another 11 miles[637] before reaching the northern shore of the Sea of Galilee. Today, as in the first century, the river travels 14 miles[638] through the Sea of Galilee, then meanders an additional 200 miles[639] until it empties into the Dead Sea. During its 240-mile[640] course southward over descending terrain, the Jordan drops close to half a mile[641] in elevation, from 1,000 feet[642] above sea level to 1,385 feet[643] below sea level at the shore of the Dead Sea, the lowest exposed land on Earth.

Map: Jordan River

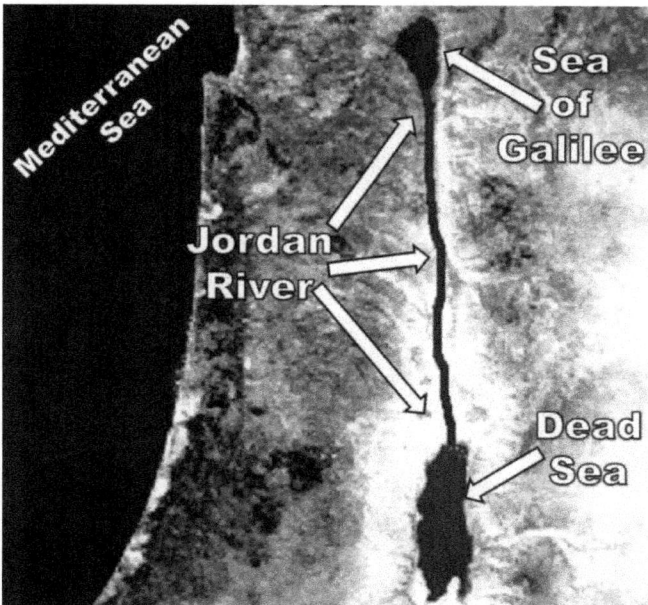

Figure 8 - 15

---

[636] Six kilometers
[637] 18 kilometers
[638] 23 kilometers
[639] 322 kilometers
[640] 387 kilometers
[641] 0.8 kilometers
[642] 305 meters
[643] 422 meters

Jordan River: North of Sea of Galilee (1931 A.D.)

Figure 8 - 16

Jordan River: Flowing into Sea of Galilee (1931 A.D.)

Figure 8 - 17

Jordan River: Flowing Out of Sea of Galilee (1931 A.D.)

Figure 8 - 18

Jordan River: South of Sea of Galilee (About 1920 A.D.)

Figure 8 - 19

Jordan River: Winding Southward to Dead Sea (1931 A.D.)

Figure 8 - 20

Jordan River: Flowing into Dead Sea (1931 A.D.)

Figure 8 - 21

Acknowledging Their Sins (Matthew 3:6)

Those who responded to John's message from God did so "acknowledging their sins" as he submerged them in the water.[644] The Greek word translated "acknowledging" is *exomologoúmenoi* (ĕx-ŏm-ŏl-ŏg-ŏú-mĕ-nŏï).[645] Even though many translators render the term as "confessing," precisely it means "acknowledging; revealing knowledge of, demonstrating awareness of, recognizing the existence of."

***

Contemplation Points

1. When did believers immersed by John acknowledge their sins?
   a. Before entering the water?
   b. After entering the water?
2. How did they acknowledge their sins?
   a. Silently to God?
   b. Verbally?
   c. Privately, to the person immersing them?
   d. Publicly, so all present could hear?
3. How specifically did they acknowledge their sins?
4. In regard to the questions listed above,
   a. Did you use the Scriptures as the source of your answer? If so, which Scriptures?
   b. Did you utilize the traditions of men as the source for your answer? If so, explain why?
   c. If the Scriptures do not provide the answers, how would that affect your actions?

---

[644] Matthew 3:6 BT
[645] *Exomologoúmenoi* (ĕx-ŏm-ŏl-ŏg-ŏú-mĕ-nŏï), ἐξομολογούμενοι

Review of Matthew's Text (Matthew 3:1-6)

1 Now, in those days, John the Immerser came proclaiming in the Judean Desert, saying, 2 "Repent, for the Kingdom of the Heavens has come near." 3 For this was he who was spoken of through the prophet, Isaiah, saying, "A voice crying aloud in the desert, 'Prepare the Lord's way. Make His paths straight.'"

4 Now, John, himself, wore camel hair clothing, together with a skin belt around his waist. And his food was locusts and wild honey. 5 Jerusalem and all Judea, as well as the entire region around the Jordan, came out to him. 6 And, they were immersed in the Jordan River by him, acknowledging their sins. (BT)

CHAPTER 9

....

Poisonous Snakes: Pharisees & Sadducees

The Pharisees and Sadducees, sharply at odds with each other, may have surprised John by showing up together. They had ventured from the city far into the wilderness "for his immersion,"[646] an unusual outing for either of those groups. John did not welcome them.

Matthew's Text (Matthew 3:7-12)[647]

7 Now, seeing many of the Pharisees and Sadducees coming for his immersion, he said to them, "Brood of poisonous snakes. Who warned you[648] to flee from the anger that is to come? 8 Produce fruit consistent with repentance. 9 And do not think of saying to yourselves, 'We have Abraham as our father.' Because, I say to you that God is able to raise up children to Abraham from these stones. 10 The axe is already being stretched out toward the

---

[646] Matthew 3:7 BT

[647] Mark 1:7-8 and Luke 3:7-18 parallel Matthew 3:7-12.

[648] To convey the intent of Matthew's Greek text, the BT marks *you* and *your* with a double underscore when plural (i.e., you, your).

*root of the trees. Every tree not producing good fruit is being
chopped down and thrown into the fire."*

*11 "Indeed, I immerse you in water into repentance. Yet,
the One coming after me is mightier than I am. I am not worthy
enough to put away His sandals. He will immerse you in the Holy
Spirit and fire. 12 With the winnowing fork in His hand, He will
thoroughly clear His threshing floor and gather His wheat into the
storehouse. However, He will burn the chaff in inextinguishable
fire."* (BT)

Who Were the Pharisees? (Matthew 3:7)

John the Immerser encountered "many of the Pharisees ... coming for his
immersion."[649] The Greek word rendered "Pharisee" is *Pharisaíos* (făr-ĭs-
ắĭ-ŏs),[650] a Greek transliteration of the Hebrew word *pharósh* (făr-ŏsh),[651]
which means "one who is separated." Pharisees endeavored to separate
themselves from spiritual impurities. Their sect consisted primarily of
scholars, scribes, and nonprofessionals from the lower economic middle
class. During Jesus' time on Earth they numbered about 6,000. (Josephus,
1977, p. 358)[652] A number of priests allied with the Pharisees,[653] although
most aligned with the Sadducees,[654] and some priests affiliated with no
sect.

Separatists

To remove spiritual impurities from one's life is a noble endeavor.
However, Pharisees mistakenly believed strict adherence to the religious

---

[649] Matthew 3:7 BT; These Pharisees came intending for John to immerse them. Take care
not to confuse them with the *priests* and *Levites* sent earlier by the Jews to determine
whom John claimed to be (John 1:19-28; Note verses 19 and 24).

[650] *Pharisaíos* (făr-ĭs-ắĭ-ŏs), Φαρισαῖος

[651] *Pharósh* (făr-ŏsh), פרוש

[652] *The Antiquities of the Jews*, Book 17, Chapter 2, Paragraph 4; Titus Flavius Josephus (jō-
sě-fəs), a Jewish general and historian, lived 37-100 A.D. For more information regarding
Josephus, see "Appendix 3: Glossary."

[653] John 1:19,24

[654] For more information concerning the Sadducee sect, see "Chapter 9 – Poisonous Snakes:
Pharisees & Sadducees," heading "Who Were the Sadducees? (Matthew 3:7)."

traditions fabricated by their ancestors kept them spiritually pure and they refused to associate with anyone who did not observe their customs. For that reason, the Pharisees criticized Jesus harshly for mixing with common folk.[655]

Pharisee leaders believed they had a right to assume religious authority due to their advanced education and pious behavior. They encouraged development of synagogues across the world as an act of protest against their rivals, the Sadducees, who controlled all activities related to the Temple in Jerusalem.

Interpretations

Pharisees had a strong, sound conviction that God exercised ultimate control. They correctly understood humans as spirit beings dwelling in physical bodies and believed in the resurrection of the dead.

Nevertheless, Pharisees thought numerous texts of Scripture fell short of practical application due to lack of detailed explanation. To supplement those Scriptures, Pharisees developed their own *interpretations* of those passages.[656] Pharisees alleged their interpretations clarified essential elements of God's commands. For example, one series of interpretations involved Sabbath-day activities.

The Sabbath

Sabbath Traditions

God commanded Israelites to rest each Sabbath day, the seventh day of the week, performing no labor.[657] Pharisees, convinced the Scriptures supplied insufficient clarity regarding what constitutes work, developed minutely detailed lists of deeds they could perform on the Sabbath, as well as activities they could not perform. Adhering rigidly to those traditions, they condemned anyone who did not conform to their specifications.

---

[655] Matthew 9:9-13; Mark 2:14-17; Luke 5:27-32
[656] 2 Peter 1:20-21
[657] Exodus 20:8-11; 31:15-17

For instance, God did not stipulate how far a person could walk on the Sabbath, so the Pharisees took it upon themselves to resolve the issue. They decided to allow a traveling distance of 2,000 cubits,[658] a little over half a mile,[659] on Sabbath days. Hence, Luke referred to the distance between Jerusalem and the Mount of Olives as "a Sabbath day's journey."[660]

God's List?

Why did God not provide an explicit list of approved or prohibited Sabbath-day activities? Most likely, He thought people should naturally know if their activity amounted to work or not.

Work is work. Rest is rest (not work), but does not always imply inactivity. Jesus illustrated the nature of activities God permitted on Sabbath days. He attended a dinner at a Pharisee leader's house on a Sabbath, together with other invited guests.[661] He taught that God did not forbid, but encouraged doing good deeds on the Sabbath,[662] such as rescuing a human or an animal from harm,[663] or leading a thirsty animal to water.[664] Furthermore, Jesus did not hesitate to heal sick people on the Sabbath.[665]

Although God did not provide an exhaustive list of forbidden Sabbath activities, the Scriptures identify several examples of work for the Israelites to avoid on the Sabbath,[666] including

---

[658] No absolute standard survived the ages to confirm the exact length of a Jewish cubit. Originally, the length of the forearm marked a cubit, typically from the tip of the elbow to the end of the middle finger, approximately 18 inches (46 centimeters). However, during Jesus' time on Earth, the traditional Jewish *sacred* cubit measured six handbreadths, again around 18 inches (46 centimeters), with a handbreadth typically extending across the base of the four fingers, about three inches (7.6 centimeters).

[659] 0.9 kilometers

[660] Acts 1:12 NASU

[661] Luke 14:1,7

[662] Matthew 12:11-12

[663] Luke 14:5; Matthew 12:11-12

[664] Luke 13:15

[665] Matthew 12:10,13; Luke 13:10-14; 14:2-4; John 9:14,16

[666] God permitted priests to burn sacrifices on the Sabbath (Numbers 28:1-10; Note verses 9-10.)

- Pursuing business-related activities[667]
- Carrying any kind of heavy load requiring strenuous effort[668]
- Gathering firewood.[669]

God granted the Israelites a day of rest each week, free of laborious endeavors. Thus, Jesus proclaimed, "The Sabbath was made for man, and not man for the Sabbath."[670]

Jesus Condemned Religious Traditions of Men

Obsessed with religious rituals of their own invention, Pharisees embedded their customs deeply into daily life. Teaching the hundreds of regulations accumulated from ancestors as actual laws of God, they imposed burdensome, man-made statutes on the general population. Worse yet, the Pharisees' theology[671] taught that if a conflict surfaced between their religious tradition and the Scriptures, their tradition should take precedence.[672] Jesus strongly condemned the nature of the Pharisees' religious thought and practice.[673]

***

Contemplation Points

1. Do religious leaders exist today who bind man-made traditions as though laws of God? If so, give specific examples of those traditions.
2. What counsel would Jesus give those religious leaders?
3. What counsel would Jesus give you about following such religious leaders?

---

[667] Nehemiah 10:31
[668] Jeremiah 17:21-22
[669] Exodus 35:3
[670] Mark 2:27 NASU
[671] For a definition of "theology," see "Appendix 3: Glossary."
[672] Matthew 15:1-9; Mark 7:1-13
[673] Matthew 15:1-9; 16:6-12; 23:13-33; Mark 7:1-13; 8:15; Luke 12:1

Who Were the Sadducees? (Matthew 3:7)

In addition to Pharisees, John encountered "many of the ... Sadducees coming for his immersion."[674] The Greek word rendered "Sadducee" is *Saddoukaíos* (säd-dŏu-kä-ĭ́-ŏs).[675] The first part of the word, *Saddouk*, is a Greek transliteration of the Hebrew word *tsadák* (tsä-dák),[676] which means "to be right." Hence, a Sadducee viewed himself as a *righteous one*. Although their sect numbered less than the Pharisees, the Sadducees controlled all Temple activities in Jerusalem, basing their religious authority on social position and family lineage.

Most Sadducees came from powerful aristocratic or priestly families, but many had a merchant background. Even so, not all Jewish priests affiliated with the Sadducees, for some allied with the Pharisees,[677] while others chose not to identify with any sect. As religious representatives of the upper economic class, Sadducees cultivated favorable relations with the Roman government.

Sadducees believed Moses wrote the only divinely inspired Scriptures, the set of books sometimes referred to as the Torah or the Pentateuch (Genesis, Exodus, Leviticus, Numbers, and Deuteronomy). That conviction placed the Sadducees at odds with the Pharisees, who believed God inspired the writings of all prophets. Sadducees also rejected the Pharisaic scribes'[678] teaching that religious tradition superseded the authority of the Scriptures.

Sadducees did not believe in the existence of angels or that humans are spirit beings.[679] A Sadducee viewed himself as merely another physical creature of God's fabrication. He believed Earth served as his final destiny,

---

[674] Matthew 3:7 BT; These Sadducees arrived expecting John to immerse them. Take care not to confuse them with the *priests* and *Levites* sent earlier by the Jews to determine whom John claimed to be (John 1:19-28; Note verses 19 and 24).

[675] *Saddoukaíos* (säd-dŏu-kä-ĭ́-ŏs), Σαδδουκαῖος

[676] *Tsadák* (tsä-dák), צדק

[677] John 1:19,24; For more information concerning Pharisees, see "Chapter 9 – Poisonous Snakes: Pharisees & Sadducees," heading "Who Were the Pharisees? (Matthew 3:7)."

[678] For more information concerning scribes, see "Chapter 4 – The Magi Meet Herod, King of Judea," heading "Who Were the Scribes? (Matthew 2:4)."

[679] Acts 23:8

denying the legitimacy of resurrection from the dead.[680] Jesus strongly condemned the teachings of the Sadducees.[681]

Brood of Poisonous Snakes (Matthew 3:7)

"Brood of poisonous snakes," chided John the Immerser as he confronted the Sadducees and Pharisees. John had the faith and character to go head-to-head with the most powerful religious sects of the Jews. Those two-faced teachers learned they could not hide their hypocrisy from the desert prophet.

The image of a serpent symbolized wickedness, and describing a person as the offspring of a snake amounted to calling him a son of the Devil.[682] Employing this dramatic figure of speech, John accused the Pharisees and Sadducees of poisoning the minds of Israel, just as Satan had misled Eve in the beginning.[683] Although Sadducees and Pharisees opposed one another as bitter rivals, John identified both sects as having the same venomous nature. John assessed the Jewish leaders accurately, for Jesus, too, unapologetically called them, "Brood of poisonous snakes."[684]

Anger that Is to Come (Matthew 3:7)

John the Immerser dealt two verbal blows to the Pharisees and Sadducees who had come "for his immersion."[685] First, he exposed their character, calling them, "Brood of poisonous snakes."[686] Second, in disgust he challenged, "Who warned _you_ to flee from the anger that is to come,"[687] referring to the divine indignation of our Creator, who will sentence the

---

[680] Matthew 22:23; Mark 12:18; Luke 20:27; Acts 23:8

[681] Matthew 16:6-12

[682] 2 Corinthians 11:3; Revelation 12:9; 20:2

[683] Genesis 3:1-14

[684] Matthew 12:34-38 BT; 23:33 BT

[685] Matthew 3:7 BT; These Pharisees and Sadducees arrived expecting John to immerse them. Take care not to confuse them with the *priests* and *Levites* sent earlier by the Jews to determine whom John claimed to be (John 1:19-28; Note verses 19 and 24).

[686] Matthew 3:7 BT

[687] Matthew 3:7 BT

unrepentant to eternal punishment.[688]

Fruit Consistent with Repentance (Matthew 3:8-9)

"Produce fruit consistent with repentance," John scolded the Sadducees and Pharisees.[689] Although John proclaimed "a *penitent* immersion into the forgiveness of sins,"[690] the Pharisees and Sadducees had not come to change their hypocritical ways. Instead, they planned to acquire praise from the people by making a public display of their submission to the country prophet's immersion.

Consider how Jesus portrayed the primary motivation of those egotistical religious leaders.

- "So then, when you practice kindness, do not sound a trumpet in front of you as, indeed, the hypocrites do in the synagogues and in the streets, **so that they might be praised by men**."[691]
- "And when you pray, do not be like the hypocrites; because they love to pray standing in the synagogues and on the street corners, **so that they might be noticed by men**."[692]
- "When you fast, do not put on a sad face like the hypocrites do. They disfigure their faces while fasting, **so that they might be noticed by men**."[693]
- **"They do all their works in order to be noticed by people**. For they widen their phylacteries and enlarge their tassels. Also, they love the reclining place of honor at banquets, and the preeminent seats in the synagogues, and the greetings in the markets, and to be called Rabbi by people."[694]

The Sadducees and Pharisees did gain the attention of the people that day, not through the popular praise they craved, but by way of the

---

[688] Daniel 12:2; Matthew 10:28; 25:41-46; John 5:28-29; Romans 1:18; 2:5-9; Ephesians 5:6; Colossians 3:6; 1 Thessalonians 1:10; 5:2-9; 2 Thessalonians 1:6-10

[689] Matthew 3:8 BT; Luke 3:8; Acts 26:20

[690] "A penitent immersion into the forgiveness of sins" translates precisely from the Greek text.; Mark 1:4 BT and Luke 3:3 BT

[691] Matthew 6:2 BT

[692] Matthew 6:5 BT

[693] Matthew 6:16 BT

[694] Matthew 23:5-7 BT

public humiliation brought on by John's reprimand.

***

Contemplation Points

1. Define "fruit consistent with repentance."
2. How have you produced "fruit consistent with repentance?"

Abraham as Our Father (Matthew 3:9)

"Produce fruit consistent with repentance," chastised John.[695] The Pharisees and Sadducees did not respond favorably to his rebuke, deeming themselves righteous because they descended from Abraham, a virtuous man.[696] They referred to Abraham as their "father," mistakenly thinking they inherited righteousness through his bloodline and therefore deserved special recognition from God. Thus they took exception to John's assertion that *they* needed to repent of their sins.

They scoffed under their breath at John's statement, blazing denial in their haughty eyes. Anticipating their contempt, John countered, "And do not think of saying to yourselves, 'We have Abraham as our father.'"[697]

These Stones (Matthew 3:9)

Drawing attention to the pebbles and boulders lying on the banks of the Jordan River, John emphasized the irrelevance of family ancestry to righteousness.[698] The bloodline of the Sadducees and Pharisees had no more significance than the rocks on the ground. John declared that God had the power to create human beings bearing Abraham's DNA from those lifeless stones.

John did not employ a hyperbole.[699] Bear in mind the infinite power of God. He created Adam from the dirt of the ground[700] and Eve

---

[695] Matthew 3:8 BT; Luke 3:8; Acts 26:20

[696] For more information concerning Abraham, see "Chapter 2 – Kings & Scoundrels: Jesus' Ancestors," heading "Abraham (Matthew 1:1)."

[697] Matthew 3:9 BT

[698] Acts 10:34; Romans 2:9-11; 9:6-8; Colossians 3:25; 1 Peter 1:17

[699] A hyperbole uses extravagant exaggeration to emphasize a point. For more information regarding hyperbole, see "Appendix 3: Glossary."

[700] Genesis 2:7

from one of Adam's ribs.[701] With a mere thought, He could have turned the rocks at John's feet into descendants of Abraham.

Rock-Strewn Jordan River

Figure 9 - 1

I Immerse You in Water into Repentance (Matthew 3:11)

"Produce fruit *consistent* with repentance,"[702] John reprimanded the Pharisees and Sadducees who had come "for his immersion."[703] John taught "a *penitent* immersion into the forgiveness of sins"[704] and refused to immerse them because they demonstrated no intent to change their manner of thought or behavior. He knew this "brood of poisonous snakes"[705] well.

The symbolism of John's immersion parallels the death, burial, and resurrection imagery explained by Jesus' apostle Paul to the Roman

---

[701] Genesis 2:22

[702] Matthew 3:8 BT; Luke 3:8; Acts 26:20

[703] Matthew 3:7 BT

[704] "A penitent immersion into the forgiveness of sins" translates precisely from the Greek text.; Mark 1:4 BT and Luke 3:3 BT

[705] Matthew 3:7 BT

Christians.[706] Those whom John submerged "were immersed in the Jordan River by him, *acknowledging their sins*."[707] When immersed, they died to their old way of thinking, buried their sinful lifestyle, and rose from the water to a changed life.

John protested the impenitence of the Sadducees and Pharisees as he emphasized, "Indeed, I immerse you in water *into* repentance."[708] He then warned of the fiery judgment awaiting them.

Not Worthy to Put Away His Sandals (Matthew 3:11)

In ancient cultures, an unskilled house-slave ranked lowest among servants and performed the most menial tasks. Offering a humble greeting, he retrieved the soiled outer garments of the returning master. Removing the slaveholder's sandals, he then cleaned the street grime from the master's feet. Having prepared his master to enter the residence, the house-slave would "put away his sandals,"[709] stowing the footwear until needed.

Although John the Immerser compared himself to a house-slave, he remained keenly aware God had assigned him a notable role,[710] to prepare the minds and hearts of the Jews for the Messiah's arrival. Positioning himself as one "not worthy enough to put away His sandals,"[711] John emphasized the ultimate supremacy of Jesus, the Anointed One. "I am not the Christ,"[712] he declared to those who might exalt him too highly.[713] "I am a voice of one crying in the wilderness, 'Make straight the way of the Lord.'"[714] "He must increase, but I must decrease."[715]

---

[706] Romans 6:3-7

[707] Matthew 3:6 BT

[708] Matthew 3:11 BT

[709] Matthew 3:11 BT

[710] Matthew 11:11; Luke 7:28

[711] Matthew 3:11 BT

[712] For more information about the words Messiah and Christ, see "Chapter 2 – Kings & Scoundrels: Jesus' Ancestors," heading "Christ (Matthew 1:1)."

[713] John 1:20 NASU

[714] John 1:23 NASU; Isaiah 40:3-5; For additional information concerning John's statement, see "Chapter 8 – The Desert Prophet," heading "Make His Paths Straight (Matthew 3:3)."

[715] John 3:30 NASU

He Will Immerse You in the Holy Spirit and Fire (Matthew 3:11)

"The One coming after me is mightier than I am,"[716] John announced.

Among his listeners stood priests and Levites[717] sent to determine who he claimed to be.[718] Impenitent Pharisees and Sadducees arrived expecting John to immerse them.[719] Tax collectors and soldiers came seeking spiritual guidance.[720]

The crowd desperately inquired, "What shall we do?"[721]

To that diverse throng John proclaimed, "The One coming after me … will immerse you[722] in the Holy Spirit and fire."[723]

Misunderstanding "With" Versus "In"

Some translations incorrectly render John's statement something similar to, "He will baptize you *with* the Holy Spirit and *with* fire," instead of translating it precisely as John explained, "He will immerse[724] you *in* the Holy Spirit and fire" (BT). The Greek word mistakenly translated by many as "with" in Matthew 3:11 is *en* (ĕn).[725] *En* literally means "in."

In a minority of passages, rendering *en* literally as "in" does not

---

[716] Matthew 3:11 BT

[717] Levites, descendants of Levi but not of Aaron's bloodline, served as assistants to the priests, Levites of Aaron's bloodline. Under the direction of the priests, the non-priest Levites cared for the mundane needs of God's Temple (See 1 Chronicles 6:48; 23:3-6,26-32). For additional information regarding Levites, see "Appendix 3: Glossary".

[718] John 1:19,24

[719] Matthew 3:7; Take care not to confuse these Pharisees and Sadducees, who arrived expecting John to immerse them, with the *priests* and *Levites* sent in John 1:19 to determine whom John claimed to be.

[720] Luke 3:12-14

[721] Luke 3:10 NASU

[722] To convey the intent of Matthew's Greek text, the BT marks *you* and *your* with a double underscore when plural (i.e., you, your).

[723] Matthew 3:11 BT

[724] For a discussion of the word "immerse" versus the word "baptize," see "Chapter 8 – The Desert Prophet," heading "They Were Immersed (Matthew 3:6)."

[725] *En* (ĕn), ἐν

communicate the intent of the writer, although it properly accomplished the writer's purpose in Greek. When addressing contexts in which proper English grammar demands that a translator not render *en* literally as "in," English grammar allows the translator to substitute words such as "on, by, with, and among." One such passage is Matthew 2:6, where English grammar requires *en* to be rendered "among," – "And you Bethlehem of the land of Judah, you are not at all least *among* the leaders of Judah" (BT).

In spite of the liberty to replace "in" with "on, by, with, among, etc." in certain contexts,[726] such substitutions should take place only when English grammar does not support the use of "in," the literal meaning of *en*. The Matthew 3:11 context does *not* require a translator to render *en* as anything other than "in." To translate *en* as "with" compromises the logical integrity of the passage, for one never immerses an object *with* something, but always immerses an object *in* something.

Glorious implications flow from Jesus' immersion of repentant believers in the Holy Spirit. However, John announced a two-fold promise with reference to Jesus, an immersion in the Holy Spirit and an immersion in fire. An examination of the context[727] of John's statement reveals the contrasting purposes of the two immersions.

---

[726] Context, the communication before and after a word or passage, often sheds light on the meaning intended by the writer or speaker.

[727] Context, the communication before and after a word or passage, often sheds light on the meaning intended by the writer or speaker.

Immerse You in the Holy Spirit (Matthew 3:11)

Extending a hand toward the penitent, John proclaimed an encouraging message of pardon. God allowed them to be buried in *water*[728] as they died to their old way of life,[729] receiving His "immersion into the forgiveness of sins."[730] Furthermore, John promised Jesus would immerse the repentant in the *Holy Spirit* one day.[731]

Shortly before His ascent to Heaven, Jesus promised His apostles He would immerse *them* in the Holy Spirit.[732] He explained the immersion would occur "not many days from now" and instructed them not to leave Jerusalem until it took place.[733] Jesus' promise to His apostles corresponded with John's former proclamation to the multitude, for the apostles formed a subset of the many penitent believers whom Jesus would immerse in the Holy Spirit.

Immerse You in Fire (Matthew 3:11)

Stretching forth the other hand toward those who did *not* "produce fruit consistent with repentance," John announced Jesus would one day immerse them in *fire*.[734] Having alerted the unrepentant Sadducees and Pharisees that, "The axe is already being stretched out toward the root of the trees. Every tree not producing good fruit is being cut off and thrown into the *fire*,"[735] John warned of the "inextinguishable *fire*"[736] awaiting those who refuse to repent of their sinful deeds. Throughout the Scriptures, God used the figure of fire, and at times literal fire,[737] to express His

---

[728] Matthew 3:11

[729] The symbolism of John's immersion parallels the death, burial, and resurrection imagery explained by the apostle Paul to the Roman Christians (Romans 6:3-7).

[730] "Immersion into the forgiveness of sins" translates precisely from the Greek text.; Mark 1:4 BT and Luke 3:3 BT

[731] Matthew 3:11

[732] Acts 1:4-9

[733] Acts 1:4-5 NASU

[734] Matthew 3:7-8,11

[735] Matthew 3:10 BT

[736] Matthew 3:12 BT

[737] Genesis 19:24-25; Jude 6-7; Leviticus 10:1-2; Numbers 11:1-2; 16:35

judgment and punishment of those who ignore His directives.[738] Hence, John forewarned his impenitent listeners of their impending immersion – in *fire*.

Misunderstandings

Some religious guides have required their followers to walk through literal fire, referring to that action as Jesus' immersion in fire. A few leaders have branded the ears of their devotees with red-hot irons, claiming to have so exercised Jesus' immersion in fire.

Others have taught that John used a grammatical structure called *hendiadys,*[739] in which two nouns joined by "and" express the emphasis more commonly communicated by a noun plus an adjective. For example, Paul utilized a hendiadys when he explained that Jesus "gave some as apostles, and some as prophets, and some as evangelists, and some as pastors and teachers."[740] Although Paul separated the roles into *four* groups beginning with the word "some,"[741] he listed *five* nouns (apostles, prophets, evangelists, pastors, teachers). Following the fourth "some," he employed a Greek hendiadys, intending "teachers" to modify "pastors." Thus, when he wrote, "And some as *pastors and teachers*," Paul conveyed the thought, "And some as *teaching pastors*."

Claiming John used a hendiadys, a few incorrectly translate his statement as "He will immerse you in the fiery Holy Spirit," instead of accurately translating it, "He will immerse you in the Holy Spirit and fire" (BT). They mistake the word "fire" to modify the word "Spirit." However, the context of John's statement does not support the notion of a hendiadys. He utilized the *fire* figure to emphasize the unfavorable outcome awaiting the impenitent.

---

[738] Exodus 15:7; Deuteronomy 4:23-24; Psalm 11:6; 97:3-5; Isaiah 4:2-4; 5:24-25; 30:27; 33:11-14; 47:12-14; Ezekiel 38:22; Malachi 3:2-5; Matthew 13:40-42; 25:41; Luke 12:49; John 15:6; Hebrews 12:25-29

[739] Hendiadys (hĕn-dī-ə-dĭs); For additional information regarding hendiadys, see "Appendix 3: Glossary."

[740] Ephesians 4:11 NASU

[741] Some translations insert "the" instead of "some."

The Context[742]

In the four verses immediately preceding his assertion that Jesus "will immerse you[743] in the Holy Spirit and fire," John expressed God's disfavor with the unrepentant.

- "Brood of poisonous snakes. Who warned you to flee from the anger that is to come?" (Matthew 3:7 BT)
- "Produce fruit consistent with repentance." (Matthew 3:8 BT)
- "Do not think of saying to yourselves, 'We have Abraham as our father.' Because, I say to you that God is able to raise up children to Abraham from these stones." (Matthew 3:9 BT)
- "The axe is already being stretched out toward the root of the trees. Every tree not producing good fruit is being chopped down and thrown into the *fire*." (Matthew 3:10 BT)

John introduced the judgment figure of *fire* by forewarning the Pharisees and Sadducees, "Every tree not producing good fruit is being chopped down and thrown into the *fire*."[744] Immediately thereafter, he declared to the crowd of penitent followers mixed with hypocritical Pharisees and Sadducees, "He will immerse you in the Holy Spirit and *fire*."[745]

---

[742] Context, the communication before and after a word or passage, often sheds light on the meaning intended by the writer or speaker.

[743] To convey the intent of Matthew's Greek text, the BT marks *you* and *your* with a double underscore when plural (i.e., you, your).

[744] Matthew 3:10 BT

[745] Matthew 3:11 BT

Unproductive Olive Trees Prepared for the Fire (About 1934 A.D.)

Figure 9 - 2

His Threshing Floor (Matthew 3:12)

John next compared the two contrasting immersions to a threshing floor. Harvesters used a threshing floor to separate useless chaff from wholesome grain. A worker spread sheaves of wheat, barley, or flax over a path trod by oxen or donkeys. The animals trampled the stalks as they walked in a circle, sometimes pulling a sledge behind them, on which a laborer stood as he drove the animals forward. The weight of the sledge and animals crushed the heads of the plants, separating the kernels of grain from their husks.

The laborer then disposed of the chaff, any part of the plant other than the grain. Scooping up the mixed grain and chaff with a winnowing fork,[746] he threw the load into the air. The grain fell to the ground in a pile, while the lighter chaff blew to the side in a heap, which the worker would later set on fire.

---

[746] Winnowing fork – a type of pitchfork

With that metaphor,[747] John explained the *desirable* result of being immersed in the Holy Spirit by Jesus and the *catastrophic* result of being immersed in fire by Jesus.[748] Regarding the penitent, John said Jesus "will gather His wheat into the storehouse,"[749] saving those He immerses in the Holy Spirit. However, concerning the impenitent, John said Jesus "will burn the chaff in inextinguishable fire,"[750] condemning those He immerses in fire.

John's listeners understood that, as metaphors, threshing and winnowing represented the separation of bad from good. Thus, they recognized the significance of John's message when he stated Jesus "will immerse you in the Holy Spirit and fire."[751] Jesus will sort out the penitent from the impenitent, just as the laborer removed the nutritious grain from the worthless chaff, saving the grain and burning the chaff.

Threshing Sledge (About 1937 A.D.)[752]

Figure 9 - 3

---

[747] A metaphor, a figure of speech, describes a characteristic or action of one noun (person, place, or thing) by replacing it in a sentence with a second *dissimilar* noun, suggesting a similarity between the two nouns. For more information about metaphors, see "Glossary."

[748] Matthew 3:12

[749] Matthew 3:12 BT

[750] Matthew 3:12 BT; God consistently employed the image of chaff in His Scriptures to symbolize those who do not obey Him, those who will suffer negative consequences due to their evil deeds. For examples see Psalm 1:4; 35:4-5; Isaiah 29 5; Hosea 13:1-4; Zephaniah 2:1-2; and Malachi 4:1.

[751] Matthew 3:11 BT

[752] Image courtesy of *The Story of the Bible: Told by Living Writers of Authority*, Amalgamated Press, Farrington Street, London, 1937

Threshing Floor & Sledges (About 1896 A.D.)

Figure 9 - 4

Winnowing (1939 A.D.)

Figure 9 - 5

Review of Matthew's Text (Matthew 3:7-12)

7 Now, seeing many of the Pharisees and Sadducees coming for his immersion, he said to them, "Brood of poisonous snakes. Who warned <u>you</u> to flee from the anger that is to come? 8 Produce fruit consistent with repentance. 9 And do not think of saying to yourselves, 'We have Abraham as our father.' Because, I say to <u>you</u> that God is able to raise up children to Abraham from these stones. 10 The axe is already being stretched out toward the root of the trees. Every tree not producing good fruit is being chopped down and thrown into the fire."

11 "Indeed, I immerse <u>you</u> in water into repentance. Yet, the One coming after me is mightier than I am. I am not worthy enough to put away His sandals. He will immerse <u>you</u> in the Holy Spirit and fire. 12 With the winnowing fork in His hand, He will thoroughly clear His threshing floor and gather His wheat into the storehouse. However, He will burn the chaff in inextinguishable fire." (BT)

CHAPTER 10

....

Jesus Fulfills All Righteousness

Customarily, the oldest son in a Jewish family assumed the paternal responsibilities upon his father's death. Jesus, the eldest among a sibling group of five brothers and at least two sisters,[753] would have taken on His family's leadership after Joseph died. As head of the family, He would have trained His brothers as craftsmen,[754] just as Joseph had trained Him.

Once the family no longer required His presence, perhaps when His brothers came of age, Jesus left Nazareth to accomplish the purpose for which He had come to Earth. He had lived in Nazareth for about 30 years[755] when that heartrending day came.[756] How could He explain? Perhaps Mary understood. Uneasy questions would have spilled out of His puzzled

---

[753] Matthew 12:46; 13:53-56; Mark 6:1-4; Luke 8:19-21; John 2:12; 1 Corinthians 9:5

[754] For additional information about the craftsmen of that day, see "Chapter 3 – Birth of Jesus, Rescuer of His People," heading "Joseph (Matthew 1:18)," subheading "Joseph the Craftsman."

[755] Luke 3:23

[756] Matthew 20:18-19,28; Mark 10:45; John 10:17-18; 1 Timothy 2:5-6; Galatians 1:3-4

siblings.[757]

"Where are you going?"

"Why?"

"When will you be back?"

Having taken leave of His family, Jesus traveled southward to the village of Bethany a few miles north of the Dead Sea.

Matthew's Text (Matthew 3:13-17)[758]

<u>13</u> *Then Jesus arrived at the Jordan from Galilee to be immersed by John.*

<u>14</u> *Even so, John was stopping Him, saying, "I need to be immersed by You, and You come to me?"*

<u>15</u>[a] *Jesus answered him, "Permit it now, for it is appropriate for us to fulfill all righteousness."*

<u>15</u>[b] *Then he consented.*

<u>16</u> *After being immersed, Jesus immediately went up away from the water. And, look, the heavens were opened to Him, and He saw the Spirit of God descending like a dove and coming upon Him.*

<u>17</u> *And, listen, a Voice out of the heavens said, "This is My Son, the Beloved One, with whom I am very pleased!"* (BT)

---

[757] Matthew 13:55-56; Mark 6:3
[758] Mark 1:9-11, Luke 3:21-23, and John 1:29-34 parallel Matthew 3:13-17.

Jesus Arrived at the Jordan River (Matthew 3:13)

After traveling about 60 miles[759] southeastward from Nazareth, Jesus arrived at the small village of "Bethany beyond the Jordan."[760] Bethany, John the Immerser's operations center at that time,[761] lay on the east bank of the Jordan River, five miles[762] north of the Dead Sea and seven miles[763] southeast of Jericho.

Map: Nazareth to Bethany

Figure 10 - 1

---

[759] 97 kilometers

[760] John 1:28 NASU; John 3:26; 10:40; Take care not to confuse Bethany beyond the Jordan with the Bethany that lay on the southeastern slope of the Mount of Olives, 1.4 miles (2.2 kilometers) east of Jerusalem, where Lazarus lived with his sisters, Mary and Martha (John 11:1).

[761] John later stayed at the village of Aenon (Greek for "springs"), about 38 miles (61 kilometers) north of Bethany on the west side of the Jordan River, "because there was much water there" (John 3:23 NASU).

[762] Eight kilometers

[763] 11 kilometers

Permit It Now (Matthew 3:15)

"I need to be immersed by You, and You come to me?" John balked.

Jesus did not answer, "You're right John. I *am* more righteous than you. I'll just dunk *Myself* in the water." He refused to modify the Father's command in any way. As He later explained, "I do exactly as the Father commanded Me."[764] Jesus insisted that John immerse Him.

To Fulfill All Righteousness (Matthew 3:15)

"To fulfill all righteousness,"[765] Jesus submitted to the Father's desire that He be immersed. "I have come down from Heaven, not to do My own will, but the will of Him who sent Me,"[766] He later affirmed to a crowd by the Sea of Galilee.

The evangelists Mark and Luke both described John's immersion of his disciples as "a penitent immersion into the forgiveness of sins."[767] Yet, Jesus remained "innocent, undefiled"[768] – "without sin."[769] Why should *He* submit to John for immersion?

"Love the Lord your God with *all* your heart, with *all* your soul, with *all* your mind, and with *all* your strength," Jesus would teach.[770] Surrendering His entire being to the will of the Father, Jesus allowed John to immerse His body in the Jordan River and raise it from the water, a representation of Jesus' forthcoming death, burial, and resurrection.[771] Since Jesus "committed no sin,"[772] the significance of His immersion

---

[764] John 14:31

[765] Matthew 3:15

[766] John 6:38 BT; Matthew 26:39; Mark 14:36; Luke 22:42

[767] "A penitent immersion into the forgiveness of sins" translates precisely from the Greek text.; Mark 1:4 BT and Luke 3:3 BT

[768] Hebrews 7:26 NASU

[769] Hebrews 4:15 NASU; 2 Corinthians 5:21; 1 Peter 2:21-22; 1 John 3:5

[770] Mark 12:30 NASU

[771] The symbolism of John's immersion parallels the death, burial, and resurrection imagery explained by the apostle Paul to the Roman Christians (Romans 6:3-7).

[772] 1 Peter 2:22 NASU

extended beyond forgiveness of sins – to a demonstration of commitment "to fulfill all righteousness."[773]

***

Contemplation Point

- How have you demonstrated your commitment "to fulfill *all* righteousness?"

Spirit of God Descending (Matthew 3:16)

Of the many immersions that day,[774] the only supernatural phenomena noted by Jesus' biographers occurred after *His* immersion. "Jesus immediately went up away from the water,"[775] "and while He was praying"[776] "the heavens were opened,"[777] "and He saw the Spirit of God descending like a dove and coming upon Him."[778] John the Immerser acknowledged that he, too, "watched the Spirit coming down from heaven like a dove, and He remained on Him."[779] With that act, God anointed Jesus with the Holy Spirit.[780]

Anointing

Historical Background

Among the Israelites, anointing originated with the divinely decreed ceremony of pouring "holy anointing oil" on a person's head or on an object.[781] God specified the ingredients and proportions mixed when preparing the oil[782] and restricted use of the formula to dedicating an

---

[773] Matthew 3:15 BT
[774] Luke 3:21
[775] Matthew 3:16 BT; Mark 1:10
[776] Luke 3:21 NASU
[777] Matthew 3:16 BT; Luke 3:21; Mark 1:9-10
[778] Matthew 3:16 BT; Mark 1:10; Luke 3:22
[779] John 1:32 BT
[780] Acts 10:38; Luke 4:14-21; Acts 4:27-28
[781] Exodus 30:25-30 NASU
[782] Exodus 30:22-25

individual or item to His service.[783] The ritual signified God's assignment of a special purpose for the person or thing anointed.[784]

God commanded Moses to dedicate the Tabernacle, together with its furnishings and fixtures, utilizing the "holy anointing oil."[785] He also directed Moses to anoint Aaron and his sons with the oil as He appointed them priests.[786] Throughout the ages, high priests continued to be anointed with the oil before assuming their role.[787]

The prophet Samuel anointed Saul as king of Israel in the same way.[788] The prophet Nathan and the priest Zadok together anointed Solomon as king.[789] God also instructed the prophet Elijah to anoint Jehu as king of Israel and Elisha as a prophet.[790]

---

[783] Exodus 30:33
[784] Leviticus 8:10-12
[785] Exodus 30:25-26 NASU; Numbers 7 :1
[786] Exodus 30:30-31; 40:13-15
[787] Leviticus 21:10; Numbers 35:25
[788] 1 Samuel 9:15-17; 10:1
[789] 1 Kings 1:34
[790] 1 Kings 19:16

Anointing of Jesus

The Father of all creation assigned Jesus a momentous task when He "anointed Him with the Holy Spirit"[791] and confirmed to the world, "This is My Son, the Beloved One, with whom I am very pleased!"[792] Just as those individuals anointed previously had carried out the special responsibilities assigned them, Jesus fulfilled His unique roles of supreme

- Prophet[793]
- High Priest[794]
- King[795]
- King of kings[796]
- Lord[797]
- Lord of lords[798]
- Final sacrifice[799]
- Anointed One/Messiah/Christ.[800]

Like a Dove (Matthew 3:16)

The Spirit Descended

As the Father anointed Jesus with the Spirit, Jesus "saw the Spirit of God descending like a dove and coming upon Him."[801] The phrase "like a dove," an adverbial simile,[802] describes the *manner* in which the Spirit descended. Floating down at an angle, a dove flutters toward a landing,

---

[791] Acts 10:38 NASU; Luke 4:14-21; Acts 4:27

[792] Matthew 3:16 BT

[793] Matthew 21:11; Luke 24:19

[794] Hebrews 2:17; 4:14

[795] Luke 1:32-33

[796] 1 Timothy 6:15; Revelation 17:14; 19:16

[797] Matthew 22:43-44

[798] 1 Timothy 6:15; Revelation 17:14; 19:16

[799] Hebrews 10:11-14; 9:26

[800] Matthew 1:1

[801] Matthew 3:16 BT; Mark 1:10; Luke 3:22; John 1:32

[802] A simile, a figure of speech, describes an action or characteristic of one noun (person, place, or thing) by comparing a characteristic or action of a second *dissimilar* noun, often introducing the comparison with "like" or "as." For more information about similes, see "Appendix 3: Glossary."

hovering as it gently settles onto its resting place. The Spirit touched down on Jesus in a similar way. The passages below illustrate the manner in which the Spirit dropped from the sky.[803]

- "He saw the Spirit of God **descending** *like a dove* and coming upon Him" (Matthew 3:16 BT)
- "He saw the heavens opening, and the Spirit *like a dove* **descending** upon Him" (Mark 1:10 NASU)[804]
- "The Holy Spirit **descended** upon Him in bodily form *like a dove*" (Luke 3:22 NASU)
- "I have seen the Spirit **descending** *as a dove* out of heaven, and He remained upon Him" (John 1:32 NASU)

Luke wrote, "The Holy Spirit descended upon Him in bodily form,"[805] yet not one of the writers offered a description of its visible characteristics. Instead, fascinated with the Spirit's *mode* of entry onto the scene, they described the *way* He came down. Having assumed observable qualities, the Spirit led everyone at the river to marvel at the *manner* of His extraordinary descent.

Why Many Believe a Dove Descended

Why do many think the Holy Spirit became a dove when descending upon Jesus? They have either misunderstood the significance of the similes "like a dove" and "as a dove," or read a *paraphrased* edition of the Scriptures that mistakenly states the Spirit assumed the shape of a dove. A paraphrase employs personal commentary, rewording an author's statements instead of translating them. For instance, in Matthew 3:16 one paraphrase says, "He saw the Spirit of God coming down in the *form of a*

---

[803] The writers' Greek spelling of the words translated "like" (*hosei*, pronounced hō-sĕí, ὡσεὶ) in Matthew 3:16 and "as" (*hos*, pronounced hōs, ὡς) in Mark 1:10, Luke 3:22, and John 1:32, identifies them as *adverbial* particles denoting comparison. The *adverbial* similes "like a dove" (Matthew 3:16 BT; Mark 1:10 NASU) and "as a dove" (John 1:32 NASU) modify the present active participle "descending." In Luke 3:22 (NASU), the *adverbial* simile "like a dove" modifies the finite verb "descended."

[804] Scripture quotations marked NASU (The New American Standard Bible Update) cite the New American Standard Bible®, Copyright© 1960, 1962, 1963, 1968, 1971, 1972, 1973, 1975, 1977, 1995 by The Lockman Foundation (www.Lockman.org). Used by permission.

[805] Luke 3:22 NASU

dove,"[806] in lieu of translating precisely as Matthew wrote it, "He saw the Spirit of God *descending like a dove.*"[807]

Take care not to equate paraphrases with translations, for when reading a paraphrased edition of the Scriptures you study a *commentary*, not a translation of the words of God's prophets. Check the preface of your study Bible to determine whether it declares itself a translation or a paraphrase. A productive study of God's Scriptures requires a precise translation. Take heed when choosing a Bible, because some professed easy-to-read translations do not disclose themselves as truly hybrids (i.e., part translation and part paraphrase). Hybrids often accommodate unsound teachings by paraphrasing only select verses while translating the rest.

The Spirit Coming upon Him (Matthew 3:16)

"After being immersed, Jesus immediately went up away from the water. And, look, the heavens were opened to Him, and He saw the Spirit of God descending like a dove and *coming upon Him.*"[808] Matthew's use of the phrase "coming upon" indicates the Holy Spirit endowed Jesus with supernatural power.

Regarding this incident, Peter explained to the Roman centurion, Cornelius, "God anointed Him [Jesus] with the Holy Spirit and with *power.*"[809] Jesus promised similar empowerment to His apostles when He told them, "You will receive *power* when the Holy Spirit has *come upon* you."[810] Likewise, regarding 12 disciples in Ephesus, Luke noted, "When Paul had laid his hands upon them, the Holy Spirit *came on* them, and they began speaking with tongues and prophesying."[811]

---

[806] Matthew 3:16, *The Living Bible* (TLB), © 1971, used by permission of Tyndale House Publishers, Inc., Wheaton, IL, USA 60189

[807] Matthew 3:16 BT

[808] Matthew 3:16 BT

[809] Acts 10:38 NASU

[810] Acts 1:8 NASU

[811] Acts 19:6 NASU

Voice Out of the Heavens (Matthew 3:17)

As the Spirit settled onto Jesus, the Father confirmed, "This is My Son, the Beloved One, with whom I am very pleased!"[812] Although not the first time humans heard the Father's voice resonating,[813] and not the last,[814] it perhaps proved the most significant.

That's My Boy

The Father's exclamation concerning His son Jesus would have overflowed with emotion similar to the cheering of Billy's dad. Billy competed like a champion that unforgettable afternoon. Dad stood in the bleachers rooting him on, anxious and unable to sit. "He did it! He did it!" Dad screamed as Billy made the winning play, saving the game. Beaming at the other howling parents, Dad bellowed, "That's *my* boy!" The shouts drew Billy's glance as his father leaped among the dazzled fans. What greater content could a son or father experience?

This is My Son (Matthew 3:17)

Submitting to His Father's desire, Jesus surrendered His body to John for immersion, honoring His pledge "to fulfill all righteousness."[815] Overjoyed, the Father proclaimed to the river crowd, "This is *My* Son!"[816] His declaration validated Jesus' paternity and endorsed His authority.[817] The thundering words would have drawn Jesus' glance as the startled multitude gazed into the sky. What greater content could the Son or the Father experience?

---

[812] Matthew 3:17 BT
[813] Exodus 20:1-22
[814] Matthew 17:1-5; Luke 9:34-35; John 12:27-29; Acts 9:1-7; 2 Peter 1:17-18
[815] Matthew 3:15 BT
[816] Matthew 3:17 BT
[817] Matthew 11:27; 16:16; 17:5; 28:19-20; Mark 1:1, Luke 1:31-35; John 5:19-27; 6:40; 3:16-18; 3:35-36; 14:6-11; 17:1; 20:30-31; Hebrew 1:1-3; 1 John 1:1-3; 2:23-24

Review of Matthew's Text (Matthew 3:13-17)

13 Then Jesus arrived at the Jordan from Galilee to be immersed by John.

14 Even so, John was stopping Him, saying, "I need to be immersed by You, and You come to me?"

15ª Jesus answered him, "Permit it now, for it is appropriate for us to fulfill all righteousness."

15ᵇ Then he consented.

16 After being immersed, Jesus immediately went up away from the water. And, look, the heavens were opened to Him, and He saw the Spirit of God descending like a dove and coming upon Him. 17 And, listen, a Voice out of the heavens said, "This is My Son, the Beloved One, with whom I am very pleased!" (BT)

Epilogue

Empowered[818] by the Holy Spirit and encouraged by the Father, Jesus set out to accomplish the purpose for which He had come to Earth, to deliver us from the dreadful consequence of our defiance.[819] To our rescue came the Word of God,[820] emptying Himself of the power and privileges of God to appear as a common human infant when born on Earth.[821] Born to die,[822] Jesus would make our reconciliation with God possible by submitting Himself as a "guilt offering" on our behalf.[823]

Leaving John and the river crowd behind, Jesus turned His face toward the harsh Judean Desert where He would prepare further for the completion of His divine task.

---

[818] Acts 10:38; Luke 4:14

[819] Matthew 10:28; Matthew 13:49-50; Matthew 25:41-43,46 (Note verse 46.); Romans 2:5-11; Romans 6:23; 2 Thessalonians 1:6-10 (Note verse 9.); 2 Peter 2:4-11 (Note verse 9.); Jude 4-14 (Note verses 6-7.)

[820] Revelation 19:13

[821] Philippians 2:5-7; John 1:14

[822] Matthew 20:28; Mark 10:45; John 10:17-18

[823] Isaiah 53:10 NASU; 1 Corinthians 5:3; Hebrews 9:26-28; Hebrews 10:12; 1 Peter 2:24; 1 John 1:7

Appendix 1: 12-Year-Old Jesus in Temple

Contrary to popular tradition, Joseph and Mary did not find twelve-year-old Jesus in the Temple teaching the teachers, but listening to the teachers and asking them questions.

Unfortunately, translators have supported the legend by rendering Luke's short account regarding the episode with lack of precision. For example, the NASU (The New American Standard Bible Update) imprecisely translates a key word in Luke 2:46-47 as "answers."

> 46 *Then, after three days they found Him in the temple, sitting in the midst of the teachers, both listening to them and asking them questions.* 47 *And all who heard Him were amazed at His understanding and His* ***answers****.*

More precisely translated,[824] Luke's passage reads,

> 46 *And it happened that after three days they found Him in the Temple sitting in the midst of the teachers, listening to them and asking them questions.* 47 *And all those hearing Him were amazed at His intelligence*[825] *and* ***responses****.*[826](BT)

---

[824] For more information about the Bagby Translation, see "Appendix 2: The Bagby Translation."

[825] The Greek word translated "intelligence," *sunései* (sün-ĕ́s-ĕĭ, συνέσει), a dative singular masculine noun, means "a putting together, intelligence, intellect" (i.e., reflective thought, quickness to understand).

[826] The Greek word translated "responses," *apokrísesin* (ă-pŏk-rĭ́s-ĕ-sĭn, ἀποκρίσεσιν), a dative plural feminine noun, means "a taking apart, separation, declaration, response (of any kind)."

In verse 46, Luke states that Joseph and Mary found Jesus listening to and asking questions of the teachers (not the teachers listening to and asking questions of Jesus). Considering verse 47 in light of the context[827] of verse 46, an astute reader understands that Jesus did not provide answers to the teachers' questions of Him, but that He responded to their teaching with questions. The questions most likely prompted discussion between the teachers and Jesus. "And all those hearing Him were amazed at His **intelligence** and **responses**."

---

[827] Context, the communication before and after a word or passage, often sheds light on the meaning intended by the writer or speaker.

Appendix 2: Bagby Translation

Original Translation

The Bagby Translation (BT), an original work designed by Dr. Chuck Bagby for oral reading, demonstrates exceptional faithfulness to the Greek and Hebrew texts. When read aloud, as though telling the story in person, the BT virtually places the reader at the feet of God's prophets.

The BT does not attempt a word-for-word translation of the Greek or Hebrew, because the syntax,[828] idiomatic expressions,[829] and interjections[830] of the original language differ from ours. Rigid adherence to Greek or Hebrew syntax frequently produces unintelligible sentences in English. Furthermore, a word-for-word translation of idiomatic expressions often communicates a meaning the writer never intended. Instead of translating word for word, the BT typically conveys the literal intent of the writer by replacing idiomatic expressions with their intended meanings, while placing the word-for-word translation in a footnote. The BT also employs English syntax and contextually-equivalent English interjections in its translation.

---

[828] Syntax – the orderly system by which words form clauses, phrases, and sentences

[829] Idiomatic expression – a figure of speech whose true significance one cannot understand by accepting the literal meaning of the individual words it contains (For further clarification, see "Idiomatic Expression" in "Appendix 3: Glossary.")

[830] Interjection – a word or phrase used to exclaim, protest, or command (For illustrations, see "Interjection" in "Appendix 3: Glossary.")

"Behold" in the Bagby Translation of Greek

Biblical writers, as well as the characters within their stories, use the Greek word *idoú* (ĭd-ŏú́)[831] as an interjection[832] at critical moments of a story to draw attention to a specific item or event. *Idoú* means "look."

Some translators continuously render *idoú* as "behold," which frequently produces awkward sentences in English. Others translate *idoú* as "lo," an archaic word. Still others omit *idoú* entirely from their translation, finding it difficult to fit the word smoothly into English. None of those methods effectively expresses the varied emphasis suggested by the diverse contexts[833] in which biblical authors apply the interjection.

English has many interjections from which to choose when one desires to grasp the attention of a reader or listener. Therefore, the BT renders *idoú* in various ways to complement the variety of contexts within which biblical writers employed the word. The bullet points below contain interjections used in the BT to express the significance of *idoú* in its many contexts.

- Look
- Look here
- Look now
- See
- Observe

- Get this
- Pay attention
- Take note
- Listen

- Listen carefully
- Listen closely
- Listen now
- Listen to this

- Listen up
- Now listen
- Now listen carefully
- Now listen to this

---

[831] *Idoú* (ĭd-ŏú́), ἰδού

[832] Interjection – a word or phrase used to exclaim, protest, or command (For illustrations, see "Interjection" in "Appendix 3: Glossary.")

[833] Context, the communication before and after a word or passage, often sheds light on the meaning intended by the writer or speaker.

Kingdom of the Heavens

New Testament writers utilized both *heaven* and *heavens* synonymously to communicate exactly the same thing. In order to remain as closely parallel to the words of the original language text as practical, the Bagby Translation (BT) employs the plural *heavens* each time a biblical writer has utilized the plural form of the word (e.g., Matthew 3:2,16-17; 4:17; 5:3,10-11,16,19-20; Mark 1:10-11, John 1:51, 2 Corinthians 5:1, Ephesians 1:10, Acts 7:56; and others).

Bold Font

The BT occasionally highlights words in bold font. Although the highlights do not exist in the original language text, they help the reader follow the logical thought of particular passages. Matthew's genealogy of Jesus provides one example of the BT's use of bold font.[834]

You and Your

Readers of English frequently have difficulty determining whether a biblical writer employed the singular or plural of *you* and *your*. To convey the intent of the original language text, the BT marks *you* and *your* with a double underscore when plural (i.e., <u>you</u>, <u>your</u>).

---

[834] See "Chapter 2 – Kings & Scoundrels: Jesus' Ancestors," heading "Matthew's Text (Matthew 1:1-17)."

Church Speak

Church speak, ambiguous vocabulary in our language typically confined to *traditional* Christian religious discussion, tends to blur the exact meanings intended by biblical authors in their Greek and Hebrew texts and often leads Bible readers to misunderstand God's Scriptures. The BT avoids church speak by utilizing precise translations. The chart below presents a few examples of vocabulary employed by the BT in lieu of church speak.

CHURCH SPEAK	BAGBY TRANSLATION	PASSAGE
Baptize	Immerse	Matthew 3:11
Blessed	Fortunate Privileged	Matthew 5:3 Matthew 16:17
Confessing	Acknowledging	Matthew 3:6
Gospel	Good message Good news	Matthew 4:23 Matthew 11:5
Miracles	Supernatural acts	Matthew 7:22
Miraculous powers	Supernatural powers	Matthew 13:54
Preaching	Proclaiming	Matthew 3:1

Appendix 3: Glossary

Angel

See "Chapter 3 – Birth of Jesus, Rescuer of His People," heading "An Angel Appeared (Matthew 1:20)."

Anointing

See "Chapter 10 – Jesus Fulfills All Righteousness," heading "Spirit of God Descending (Matthew 3:16)," subheading "Anointing."

Apostle

A *transliteration* of the Greek word *apóstolos* (ä-pŏ-stŏ-lŏs), ἀπόστολος, a common Greek word describing any delegate. When *transliterating*, a translator spells out an approximation of the original language's pronunciation of a word using the alphabet of the second language. Within the Scriptures, "apostles" typically refers to the 12 followers chosen by Jesus to represent Him. For lists of the original twelve, see Matthew 10:1-4; Mark 3:13-19; Luke 6:12-16; and Acts 1:13 (which excludes Judas Iscariot, who had died).

Aramaic

Aramaic, a Semitic (i.e., Shemitic) language closely related to Hebrew, emerged through the descendants of Shem, Noah's oldest son (Genesis 5:32; Genesis 10:1,21). Shem named one of his sons Aram (Genesis 10:22-23). Around 2000 B.C., the Aramaic language began to develop through Aram's descendants, the Arameans.

By the time of the Assyrian Empire (911-612

B.C.), merchants and diplomats over all southwest Asia spoke Aramaic as their preferred professional language. Following Babylonia's conquest of Assyria, Aramaic became one of the official languages of the Babylonian Empire (612-539 B.C.).

During the Babylonian deportation, the exiled Judahites began to blend Aramaic with their native Hebrew speech, resulting in the development of a Hebrew dialect[835] of Aramaic. Due to their common linguistic origin, Hebrew and Aramaic shared alphabetic characters and contained similar vocabulary, which facilitated the evolution of the new dialect.

Following the return of the Judahites from the Babylonian deportation to their Judean homeland (538 B.C.), they continued to speak a distinct Hebrew dialect of Aramaic. During the Roman occupation of Judea, when Jesus lived on Earth, the Jews still spoke Aramaic as their first language.

Augustus

The Roman Senate appointed Caesar Augustus as the first emperor of the Roman Empire, after nearly a century of civil wars. Augustus, who ruled from 27 B.C. until his death in 14 A.D., restored unity to the empire and created an orderly government. Historians refer to that era as the *Augustan Age*. The Augustan Age brought relative peace and prosperity within most of the territories of the Roman Empire.

---

[835] Dialect – a regional style of spoken language distinguished by distinctive pronunciation, vocabulary, grammar, or any combination of the three characteristics

Babylonian Deportation	See "Chapter 2 – Kings & Scoundrels: Jesus' Ancestors," heading "The Babylonian Deportation (Matthew 1:11)."
Baptism	See "Chapter 8 – The Desert Prophet," heading "They Were Immersed (Matthew 3:6)."
Bethany Beyond the Jordan	See "Chapter 8 – The Desert Prophet," heading "Judean Desert (Matthew 3:1)," subheading "Bethany beyond the Jordan."
Camel Hair	See "Chapter 8 – The Desert Prophet," heading "Camel Hair Clothing with a Skin Belt (Matthew 3:4)," subheading "Camel Hair Clothing."
Chief Priests	See "Chapter 4 – The Magi Meet Herod, King of Judea," heading "Who Were the Chief Priests? (Matthew 2:4)."
Christ	See "Chapter 2 – Kings & Scoundrels: Jesus' Ancestors," heading "The One Called Christ (Matthew 1:1,16-17)" and "Chapter 10 – Jesus Fulfills All Righteousness," heading "Spirit of God Descending (Matthew 3:16)," subheading "Anointing."
Church Speak	See "Appendix 2: Bagby Translation," heading "Church Speak."
Circumcise	To circumcise means to surgically remove the foreskin of a penis.
Confess	See "Chapter 8 – The Desert Prophet," heading "Acknowledging Their Sins (Matthew 3:6)."
Context	Context, the communication positioned before and after a word or passage, often sheds light on the meaning intended by a writer or speaker.

Council	The Council, a man-made Jewish organization that originated during the second century B.C., had no place in any design given by God through His prophets or Scriptures. Some translations refer to the Council as the "Sanhedrin" or "Sanhedrim," both transliterations of the Greek word *sunédrion* (sun-ĕd-rĭ-ŏn, συνέδριον), which literally means "sitting together."

The Council served judicial purposes as a type of Supreme Court, yet also filled administrative roles. With the High Priest as leader, Council members came from both the Sadducee and Pharisee sects (Acts 23:6) and never numbered below 70. Members of the Council mentioned in the Scriptures include

- The High Priest and his associates, the Sadducees (Acts 5:17, 21,27),
- The chief priests, elders, and scribes (Mark 15:1),
- Gamaliel, a leader of the Pharisees (Acts 5:34),
- Nicodemus, a Pharisee (John 3:1), and
- Joseph of Arimathea (Mark 15:43, Luke 23:50).

Craftsman	See "Chapter 3 – Birth of Jesus, Rescuer of His People," heading "Joseph (Matthew 1:18)," subheading "Joseph the Craftsman."
Cubit	No absolute standard survived the ages to confirm the exact length of a Jewish cubit. Originally, the length of the forearm marked a cubit, typically from the tip of the elbow to the end of the middle finger, approximately 18 inches (46 centimeters). However, during Jesus' time on Earth, the

traditional Jewish *sacred* cubit measured six handbreadths, again around 18 inches (46 centimeters), with a handbreadth typically extending across the base of the four fingers, about three inches (7.6 centimeters).

Cuneiform
Cuneiform, a system of writing that emerged around 3100 B.C. in southern Mesopotamia within the Sumerian culture, consisted of wedged shaped strokes engraved into tablets of clay, stone, metal, or wax. Civilizations of several languages and cultures used the cuneiform style of writing over a period of about 3,000 years.

Dialect
A dialect, a regional style of speaking a language, distinguishes itself through distinctive pronunciation, vocabulary, grammar, or any combination of these three characteristics.

Genealogy
A genealogy lists a person's or family's ancestors in order of birth, sometimes in reverse order.

Genitive
In Greek grammar, the genitive case denotes possession, or a relation similar to possession, as in "the son *of* the craftsman" (Matthew 13:55 BT).

Gentile
The Jews identified Gentiles as anyone not of the bloodline of Jacob, son of Isaac, grandson of Abraham. God gave Jacob the name *Israel* (Genesis 32:28). In earlier history, Israelites treated Gentiles cordially. However, following the return of the Judahites to their homeland of Judea from the Babylonian deportation, most Jews became extremely prejudiced and hostile toward Gentiles.

Greco-Roman	The phrase "Greco-Roman" refers to something characteristic of both the ancient Greek and ancient Roman cultures.
Hebrew	Hebrew, a Semitic (i.e., Shemitic) language, emerged through the descendants of Shem, Noah's oldest son (Genesis 5:32; Genesis 10:1,21). Shem had a great-great-great grandson named Eber, sometimes spelled "Heber," through whose descendants the Hebrew language developed. Many scholars regard Eber to be the patriarch of the Hebrew race (Genesis 10:21-25, 31).
Hendiadys	A hendiadys (hĕn-dī́-ə-dĭs) utilizes a grammatical structure in which two nouns joined by "and" express the emphasis more commonly communicated by a noun plus an adjective. For example, the hendiadic sentence, "The henchman clothed himself in a *robe and black*," conveys the same message as the more ordinary sentence, "The henchman clothed himself in a *black robe*."
Herod	Historians sometimes refer to *Herod*, the given name of one of the rulers of Judea, as *Herod the Great*. *Hródas* (Hrṓ-dās, ῾Ηρώδης), the Greek word translated "Herod," means "heroic." Descendants of Herod the Great adopted the name *Herod* as their family surname.
Herodotus	Scholars refer to Herodotus, a Greek historian who lived around 485-420 B.C., as "the father of history." In *The Histories*, Herodotus wrote of events that took place during the Persian invasion of Greece in the early fifth century B.C.

Holy Anointing Oil	See "Chapter 10 – Jesus Fulfills All Righteousness," heading "Spirit of God Descending (Matthew 3:16)," subheading "Anointing."
Hyperbole	Hyperbole employs extravagant exaggeration to emphasize a point. For example, the hyperbolic statement, "Toby could eat a *mountain* of spaghetti during a single meal," conveys the same message as the more ordinary sentence, "Toby could eat a large amount of spaghetti during a single meal."
Idiomatic Expression (Idiom)	An idiomatic expression, a figure of speech sometimes referred to as "idiom," conveys a meaning impossible to understand by considering the literal sense of the individual words it contains. For example, the idiomatic expression in the sentence, "He is *pulling your leg*," expresses the same message as the more ordinary sentence, "He is *joking with you*."
Immersion	See "Chapter 8 – The Desert Prophet," heading "They Were Immersed (Matthew 3:6)."
Immersion in Fire	See "Chapter 9 – Poisonous Snakes: Pharisees & Sadducees," heading "Immerse You in the Holy Spirit and Fire (Matthew 3:11)."
Immersion in the Holy Spirit	See "Chapter 9 – Poisonous Snakes: Pharisees & Sadducees," heading "Immerse You in the Holy Spirit and Fire (Matthew 3:11)."
Interjection	An interjection, a word or phrase used to exclaim, protest, or command, may express an emotion or a reaction and may draw attention to a specific item or event. An interjection can stand alone as a part of speech (e.g., Well!; Wow!; Look!; Hey!; Oh!; No!; Listen!).

Infinitive	A verb form with no indication of person, number, mood, or tense (Examples of infinitives include *to eat, to run,* and *to swim.*)
Josephus	Titus Flavius Josephus, a Jewish general and historian, lived 37-100 A.D. He led the Judean defense when, in 66 A.D., the Roman army invaded Judea to suppress a widespread Jewish revolt. Although the Judean revolt failed, Josephus survived. He later lived in Rome, where he compiled his historical records.
Justin Martyr	Justin Martyr, born into a pagan family in the city of Flavia Neapolis some 39 miles (63 kilometers) north of Jerusalem, became a Christian during his adult years. He discussed Jesus' birth in his book, *Dialogue with Trypho,* written about 160 A.D.
Kingdom of the Heavens	See "Chapter 8 – The Desert Prophet," heading "The Kingdom of the Heavens (Matthew 3:2)."
Levites	Levites descended from Levi, third son of Jacob, the patriarch of the tribe of Levi. Levites not of Aaron's bloodline served as assistants to the priests, who descended from Aaron (Numbers 3:6-7,32). Under the direction of the priests, the non-priest Levites cared for the mundane needs of God's Tabernacle (Numbers 1:47-53; 3:5-9,23-39; 4:1-49; 7:1-9; 1 Chronicles 6:48). Upon the retirement of the Tabernacle, the Levites cared for the Temple (Ezekiel 44:9-14; Ezra 8:15-20; 1 Chronicles 23:3-6,26-32).
Linguistics	Linguistics encompasses the scientific study of the nature, structure, and historical development of languages.

Magi	See "Chapter 4 – The Magi Meet Herod, King of Judea," heading "Magi from the East (Matthew 2:1)."
Messiah	The Hebrew word *Mashíyach* (Mâ-shí-yäkh, מָשִׁיחַ), transliterated as "Messiah" in most translations of the Old Testament, means "anointed one." Messiah and Christ serve as synonyms.
Metaphor	Metaphor, a figure of speech, describes a characteristic or action of one noun (person, place, or thing) by comparing it with a second *dissimilar* noun to suggest a similarity between the two nouns. For example, the metaphor in the statement, "The truck maneuvered up the mountain on the winding *snake*," conveys the same message as the more ordinary sentence, "The truck maneuvered up the mountain on the winding *road*."
Nazarene	A Nazarene originates from the town of Nazareth.
Origen	Origen, born in Alexandria, Egypt to Christian parents, touched on the birth of Jesus in his book, *Against Celsus*, about 248 A.D.
Paraphrase	Take care not to equate *paraphrase* with a translation. A paraphrase employs personal commentary, rewording an author's statements instead of translating them. When reading a paraphrased edition of the Scriptures, you study a *commentary*, not a translation of the words written by God's prophets. Check the preface of your study Bible to determine whether it declares itself a translation or a paraphrase. A productive study of God's Scriptures requires a precise translation. Take heed when choosing a Bible, because some professed easy-to-read translations do not disclose themselves as truly hybrids (i.e., part translation

217

and part paraphrase). Hybrids often accommodate unsound teachings by paraphrasing only select verses while translating the rest.

Passover — The Passover, an annual Israelite festival, commemorated the occasion when God, through Moses, led the Israelites out of Egypt, where the Egyptians had enslaved them for hundreds of years (Exodus 12:1-32).

Pharisee — See "Chapter 9 – Poisonous Snakes: Pharisees & Sadducees," heading "Who Were the Pharisees? (Matthew 3:7)."

Pliny (the Elder) — Pliny Plinius Secundus, a first-century Roman historian and scientist, lived 23-79 A.D.

Sadducee — See "Chapter 9 – Poisonous Snakes: Pharisees & Sadducees," heading "Who Were the Sadducees? (Matthew 3:7)."

Scribes — See "Chapter 4 – The Magi Meet Herod, King of Judea," heading "Who Were the Scribes? (Matthew 2:4)."

Simile — A simile, a figure of speech, describes an action or characteristic of one noun (person, place, or thing) by comparing a characteristic or action of a second *dissimilar* noun, often introducing the comparison with "like" or "as."

Adverbial Simile

An adverbial simile modifies a verb, describing how an action occurred.
- Layla **ran** *as fast as the wind.*
- Kayley **hopped** *like a kangaroo.*
- Demos **swam** *as swiftly as a dolphin.*
- Zach **jumped** *like a frog.*

- Charlie **threw** the ball *as fast as a bullet*.
- "He saw the Spirit of God **descending** *like a dove*" (Matthew 3:16 BT).
- "He saw the heavens opening, and the Spirit *like a dove* **descending** upon Him" (Mark 1:10 NASU).
- "The Holy Spirit **descended** upon Him in bodily form *like a dove*" (Luke 3:22 NASU).
- "I have seen the Spirit **descending** *as a dove* out of heaven, and He remained upon Him" (John 1:32 NASU).

Adjective Simile

An adjective simile modifies a noun (person, place, or thing) describing a characteristic of the noun it modifies.

- Aravis' eyes are *as blue as the sky*.
- Samantha's hair is *as soft as cotton*.
- Hana's smile is *like a sunny day*.
- C.J.'s muscles are *like rock*.
- Owen's skin is *as smooth as silk*.

Strabo

Strabo, a Greek geographer, philosopher, and historian, lived from about 64 B.C.-24 A.D.

Synagogue

A synagogue, a local assembly of Jewish believers, came together on Sabbath days to worship God, sometimes with Gentile followers of God as well. Jews also referred to the building in which the assemblies took place as the *synagogue*. The Pharisees encouraged development of synagogues across the world as an act of protest against the Sadducees, who controlled all activities related to the Temple in Jerusalem. Not until sometime after 200 A.D. did Jewish tradition dictate a location inhabited by ten or more Israelite men must have a synagogue. (Unger, 1988, heading "Synagogue," subheading "Where Located")

Syntax

Syntax refers to the orderly system by which words form clauses, phrases, and sentences.

Talent

A talent, a standard measure, referred to a weight of silver. A silver talent equaled the weight of 3,000 silver shekels, or 93¾ pounds (42.5 kilograms). A gold talent amounted to double the weight of a silver talent.

Talmud

The Talmud contains traditional teachings of ancient Jewish religious scholars, not God-inspired Scripture.

Tel

Tel refers to an artificial hill created by the accumulated ruins of an ancient civilization. Over the centuries, tel mounds grew larger as successive generations built new structures on top of older remains.

Tertullian

Tertullian, the first writer to produce an extensive body of Christian literature in Latin, lived from about 160-225 A.D. in the city of Carthage, within the Roman province of Africa.

Theology

Theology, as referred to in this book, consists of any man-made system of traditions, creeds, opinions, legends, myths, or combination of these items promoted by a religious organization, denomination, or sect.

Threshing Floor   See "Chapter 9 – Poisonous Snakes: Pharisees & Sadducees," heading "His Threshing Floor (Matthew 3:12)."

Transliterate   When transliterating, instead of translating a word, a translator *spells out* an approximation of the original language's *pronunciation* of the word using the alphabet of the second language. Translators often transliterate names and words that have no corresponding term in the second language. A transliteration, having no inherent meaning of its own, derives its meaning directly from the definition of the word in the original language. If the second language contains a term carrying the same meaning as the word from the original language, no justification exists for the use of a transliteration. In that case, intellectual integrity mandates the translator employ a translation.

Wadi   Inhabitants of North Africa, the Middle East, and Southwest Asia use the term *wadi* to refer to a streambed that typically remains dry except during rainy seasons.

Worship   See "Chapter 5 – The Magi Meet Jesus, King of the Jews," heading "They Worshiped Him (Matthew 2:11)."

Appendix 4: Pronunciation Symbols

SYMBOL	PRONUNCIATION
ā	"a" as in "<u>a</u>te"
ă	"a" as in "<u>a</u>pple"
â	"a" as in "p<u>a</u>rent"
ä	"a" as in "p<u>a</u>lm"
ə	"a" as in "di<u>a</u>gram"
b	"b" as in "<u>b</u>ank"
d	"d" as in "<u>d</u>ance"
ē	"e" as in "<u>ee</u>l" "i" as in "pol<u>i</u>ce"
ě	"e" as in "l<u>e</u>t"
f	"f" as in "<u>f</u>at" "ph" as in "<u>ph</u>antom"
g	"g" as in "<u>g</u>ot"
h	"h" as in "<u>h</u>armony"
ī	"i" as in "b<u>i</u>te"
ĭ	"i" as in "b<u>i</u>t" "y" as in "ab<u>y</u>ss"
k	"k" as in "<u>k</u>iss"
kh	"ch" as in "<u>ch</u>orus"
l	"l" as in "<u>l</u>ead"
m	"m" as in "<u>m</u>any"

SYMBOL	PRONUNCIATION
n	"n" as in "<u>n</u>ot"
ngg	"ng" as in "a<u>ng</u>le"
ō	"o" as in "t<u>o</u>te"
ŏ	"o" as in "<u>o</u>bstruct"
ô	"aw" as in "<u>aw</u>kward"
p	"p" as in "<u>p</u>it"
r	"r" as in "<u>r</u>an"
s	"s" as in "<u>s</u>lick"
sh	"sh" as in "<u>sh</u>op"
t	"t" as in "<u>t</u>in"
th	"th" as in "wor<u>th</u>"
ū	"u" as in "f<u>u</u>me"
ŭ	"u" as in "p<u>u</u>p"
ü	"u" as in "cr<u>u</u>de" "oo" as in "t<u>oo</u>t"
û	"u" as in "t<u>u</u>rn"
y	"y" as in "<u>y</u>ellow"
z	"z" as in "ha<u>z</u>e"

Appendix 5: 13-Week Class Schedule

Week 1 – Read "Preface" through the end of page 16.

Week 2 – Read page 17 through the end of page 26.

Week 3 – Read page 27 through page 42a "Of the Lord."

Week 4 – Read page 42b "Call His Name Jesus" through the end of page 58.

Week 5 – Read page 59 "Province of Judea" through page 71a "Census."

Week 6 – Read page 71b "Magi from the East" through the end of page 92.

Week 7 – Read page 93 through the end of page 107.

Week 8 – Read page 108 through the end of page 116.

Week 9 – Read page 117 through the end of page 128.

Week 10 – Read page 129 through the end of page 144.

Week 11 – Read page 145 through the end of page 168.

Week 12 – Read page 169 through the end of page 188.

Week 13 – Read page 189 through the end of page 204.

References

Barnes, A. (1997). Barnes' Notes. *[Electronic Version]*. (R. Frew, Ed.) London, England, United Kingdom: Blackie & Son, Retrieved from PC Study Bible (2006) Version 4.03.002.

Edersheim, A. (1881). *Sketches of Jewish Social Life in the Days of Christ.* New York, NY, USA: James Pott & Co.

Herodotus. (1848). *Herodotus.* (H. Cary, Trans.) London, England, United Kingdom: Henry G. Bohn.

Hone, W. (1820). *The Apocryphal New Testament* (Quote comes from Wm. Hone's translation of "The Protevangelion" (a.k.a., "The Gospel of James") within his book "The Apocryphal New Testament." ed.). (W. Hone, Trans.) London, England, United Kingdom: Ludgate Hill.

Josephus, F. (1977). *The Complete Works of Flavius Josephus* (Fourteenth Printing ed.). (W. Whiston, Trans.) Grand Rapids, MI, USA: Kregel Publications.

Kitto, J. (1846). *A Cyclopaedia of Biblical Literature - Volume 1.* New York, NY, USA: Mark H. Newman.

Kitto, J. (1854). *Popular Cyclopaedia of Biblical Literature - Condensed.* Boston, MA, USA: Gould and Lincoln.

Martyr, J. (1755). *Dialogue with Trypho the Jew* (Vol. II). (H. Brown, Trans.) Oxford, England, United Kingdom: W. Jackson.

Miller, E. C. (1871). *Eastern Sketches: Notes of Scenery, Schools and Tent Life in Syria and Palestine.* Edinburgh, Scotland, United Kingdom: William Oliphant and Company.

Origen. (1869). *The Writings of Origen.* (A. Roberts, J. Donaldson, Eds., & F. Crombie, Trans.) Edinburgh, Scotland, United Kingdom: T. & T. Clark.

Pliny. (1848). *Natural History* (Vol. 1 Book VI). (J. Couch, Trans.) London, England, United Kingdom: George Barclay, Castle Street, Leicester Square.

Strabo. (1856). *The Geography of Strabo* (Vol. II). (H. Hamilton, & W. Falconer, Trans.) London, England, United Kingdom: Henry G. Bohn.

Tertullian. (1919). *Tertullian's Treatises Concerning Prayer & Concerning Baptism* (Vol. Translations of Christian Literature Series II Latin Texts). (A. Souter, Trans.) New York, New York, USA: The MacMillan Company.

Unger, M. (1988). The New Unger Bible Dictionary. *[Electronic Version].* Chicago, IL, USA: Moody Press. Retrieved from PC Study Bible (2006) Version 4.03.002.

About the Author

Evangelist

Chuck Bagby worked fulltime as an evangelist for ten years, completing foreign assignments in both Honduras and Argentina. Following that, while dedicating two decades to the business world, he continued to "do the work of an evangelist" (2 Timothy 4:5 NASU). He teaches today through *Burning Heart Bible Studies* seminars and books (www.BurningHeartBibleStudies.com).

Current Work

Chuck serves as a Consulting Professor of Biblical Studies for Nations University. Together with this, he conducts *The Jesus Story: What I Wish I Had Known* seminars. He also offers church leaders coaching in the implementation of his unique **T-E-A-M** leadership methodology.

Education

Chuck holds a PhD in biblical studies from the Theological University of America (TUA), having previously graduated from the Sunset International Bible Institute (SIBI). The University of Texas at San Antonio (UTSA) awarded him an MBA in International Business, with concentrations in international marketing and international finance. He earned a BA in Spanish Literature from the University of Missouri – Columbia.

Past Work

A former international business executive, Chuck specialized in team leadership, cross-cultural communication, and organizational turnarounds. Employing his unique **T-E-A-M** leadership methodology, he consistently transformed underperforming organizations into high-performance teams. He served on the Advisory Council of the College of Business at UTSA and on the Entrepreneurs' Roundtable at the same university. He has carried out business in Argentina, Bolivia, Canada, Chile, Colombia, El Salvador, England, Honduras, Mexico, Peru, Spain, Sweden, and Uruguay.

Special Request

Please let Chuck know something about you.
Send an e-mail to
AllForJesus@BurningHeartBibleStudies.com

www.BurningHeartBibleStudies.com
(A reader-supported work of faith)